Youth
Considers
Personal Moods

YOUTH FORUM SERIES

Titles in Print

Youth Asks, Why Bother About God?
by Alvin N. Rogness

Youth Considers "Do-It-Yourself" Religion
by Martin E. Marty

Youth Considers Marriage
by David R. Mace

Youth Considers Parents as People
by Randolph Crump Miller

Youth Considers Personal Moods
by Reuel L. Howe

Youth Considers Sex
by William E. Hulme

Titles in Preparation

Youth Considers Doubt and Frustration
by Paul L. Holmer

Youth Considers Life Goals
by Ross Snyder

Youth Considers the World of High School
by John S. Wood

Youth
Considers
PERSONAL MOODS

by
Reuel L. Howe

THOMAS NELSON & SONS

London   Camden, N. J.   Toronto

Second Printing, May, 1967

© 1966 by Reuel L. Howe

All rights reserved under International and Pan-American Conventions. Published in Camden, N. J., by Thomas Nelson & Sons and simultaneously in Toronto, Canada, by Thomas Nelson & Sons (Canada) Limited.

Library of Congress Catalog Card Number: 66-22000

Printed in the United States of America

Dedication to
Lynn C. Wright,
Educator and Friend
to me in my youth

Foreword

Written in the context of the Christian faith, this book is one in a series published by Thomas Nelson & Sons in collaboration with Church Youth Research.

The research agency, which serves as editor of this series, is known through *What Youth Are Thinking* (Smedsrud, 1961) and *Profiles of Church Youth* (Strommen, 1963). The Director, Dr. Merton Strommen, is known also for his work as Director of Research (1965-67) with Religious Education Association, an inter-faith agency serving all church groups.

The purpose of the series is to use points of established need to bring about meaningful contact between the GOSPEL of God in Jesus Christ and YOUNG PEOPLE. Underlying the total effort is a concern that youth throughout the English-speaking world can be helped to see that the Gospel of Christ is the core of life itself in all its realities.

Unique to this publication effort is the use that is made of research findings. These describe the specific need to which each book is addressed as well as the youth most concerned about this need. Thus a writer is helped to speak more directly to the actual conflicts, values, and beliefs of an important segment of youth.

The significance of this series is enhanced by the scholarship and pastoral concern of the authors. Their grasp of the fields in which each writes enables them to speak with authority, establishing the series as a basic reference in the area of youth work.

just a moment!

Buying and reading a book is always a gamble: Is it worth your money and time? Writing a book is also a gamble: Is what you have to say worth saying?

Writing a book for young people, I am told, is an even greater gamble because they do not "like to be told." We match each other at this point: I do not like telling people what to do. My aim in this book is to think along with you about moods and leave you to make your own decisions about what to think and do.

The next question is: What qualifications do you have for writing a book for and about adolescents when you are sixty years old and do not work with young people? Good question. The following are my answers:

1. I was once an adolescent myself, and writing this book has reactivated my memories of my own youth, and the moods, positive and negative, that I lived through.

2. I am living with two young people who are my own children and I have learned much from them.

3. I have studied human development and relationship all my life and have been a counselor to young people and their important people.

4. Finally, I have checked with young people as I planned and wrote this book. I am indebted to some of the young people of the Marquis Club of Christ Church Cranbrook, Bloomfield Hills, Michigan, and of the Marian High School, Birmingham, Michigan, and some others. They reviewed and discussed its overall outline, style, and purpose, and during its production discussed its content and expression. In a very real sense these young people have been co-authors and I am indebted to them.

Let me say a word about the people for whom this book is written and my attitude toward them. "Teen-ager" and "adolescent" are often used as degrading words. A discussion of such attitudes occurs later; but I must make clear immediately that these are not my attitudes. I find it pleasanter and more realistic to think of you as emerging adults: adults because you are no longer children; and emerging because you are not yet fully adults. When in this book I refer to "teen-ager" or "adolescent" I do so neutrally for purposes of identification only.

I have tried to write an honest book about moods in relation to the religious meanings of our life. The task is not easy. When I submitted part of the first draft to some young people they repudiated most of it because it was too "religious." When I submitted another draft, based on consultations with youth, to the committee of theologians who pass on the books in the Youth Forum Series, they said it was not religious enough. I have been caught in a bind between the older "religious" generation and the younger secular one. I have tried to respond to the suggestions of the older theologians and meet the needs of the young people whom I also regard as theologians because they are searching for meanings both immediate and ultimate. When

I could, I have chosen to respond to my younger friends because they are the ones who will be working out the new relationship between the Church and the world, between the meaning of life and the meaning of the gospel. I have written this book to help them find their own relation to the gospel out of their meanings and in their own terms. In doing this I believe I am following the example of Jesus Christ who spoke to people about life and not religion, who used the people's terms rather than the traditional ones.

Finally, the method of this book requires some explanation. Immediately following this preface comes a collection of thoughts by four adolescents which represents some of their life situations and their moods in relation to them. These ruminations prepare the reader for the following chapters and raise questions to which they are addressed. It is my hope that the reader will be able to identify with Jerry; his sister, Mary; Jake, his friend; and Bill, who is dating Mary.

So, let's go!

Contents

Foreword	7
Just a Moment!	9
Some sketches of us all	15
Why this book	24
Moods and what they do to you	32
What causes moods	43
Power of purposes over moods	58
Resources for dealing with moods	73
A resource you are afraid to use	84
Conclusion	95

some sketches of us all

Jerry Johnson, 16, is waiting outside his high school to be picked up by his mother

I wish Mom'd get going. She's always late. I've got to get home and over to Jake's by 4:00. . . . Wonder where Mary is . . . she's supposed to be here. . . . I'll bet Mom'll get here and Mary will be even later.

I wish Dad would let me drive the car or I could afford one of my own . . . Shucks, some guys can. . . . I hate being picked up by Mom. It's hard to act like a man when you're being carted around by a woman . . . she's always fussing over me as if I was a little kid. I wonder where she is though . . . hope nothing's happened to her. She's never had an accident . . . I don't know why . . . guess she'll be along.

There's Mary . . . wonder what she sees in that Bill Casey. He's sure a big jerk . . . seems so sure of himself. I wish I could've made that long run last Saturday in the game with Cedar High instead of Bill. Man, that was neat! Then they'd have cheered me instead of him. Me? What can I do? Dad says, though, that my day will come. I wish I could put some beef on my bones so I'd feel like a man. There are a lot of things I'd like to do but I don't know how. . . . Gee, I can't do anything.

15

Dad's a great guy but he's too darned successful for me. Who wants to live the way he does! . . . I wonder if he's ever had any kind of problems. . . . I mean, he couldn't have or he wouldn't be where he is. . . . Sure, he loves me, but I sure as hell wish he'd get off my back once in a while. Why should I let him live my life, too . . . . but I wish he had more time for me. I know he worries a lot about his job . . . competition is rough and I've heard him say there's always some younger man ready to push him out. It must be tough to be a man and have to take care of yourself, a family, and have no one to fall back on. Sometimes I like the idea of growing up . . . then again I'm not so sure. Things are getting tougher . . . and everybody's always yelling about grades. Everybody's at you . . . teachers, parents, and even a lot of kids always pushing for top grades. And there's a heck of a lot more to learn, too. Only a couple of guys from my class will be accepted by Dad's college. I guess he'll be disappointed if I don't make it. On top of all this I'm supposed to be an "all around man," member of the team, active in the clubs and stuff, and a heavy dater.

I'd like to try different things but I'm afraid I'll fail. It's all more'n I can do . . . like, I mean, the whole thing seems like a trap. . . . I'm stuck with all these problems . . . I didn't ask to be born. The whole deal gets me down . . . when I'm like this I just can't talk to anybody. I know Mary feels like this sometimes, too. She doesn't say much for days . . . she looks as if she's thinking unhappy things. She and Mom fight a lot, but she and Dad get along swell except when he and Mom gang up on her about something like going out with Bill. They think he's too old for her. She gets all upset and says they treat her like a baby.

She gets funny spells . . . like the time I found her staring into the mirror and bawling . . . she was real embarrassed. So was I . . . crying gets me down . . . but I asked her what was eating her. At first she wouldn't say . . . then she bawled again and said she was so ugly that no boy would ever marry her what with her teeth and complexion. . . . I didn't know what to say . . . she looks O.K. to me . . . she's not a bad looking girl . . . but I didn't say anything . . . she was having a good time crying and feeling sad.

Women are funny . . . I don't understand them. You never know what they're going to do. Take Janie . . . she likes to hold hands sometimes . . . other times she gets mad at me and really clams up. A couple of times I've held her real tight . . . pressed real close I could feel her against me . . . and we'd kiss. . . . I'd run my hands up and down her back, and once I felt the sides of her breasts, and then she'd break away and say that we shouldn't. Gee, it sure did feel good and I'm sure she liked it too. I'm glad she stopped, though . . . I mean, I was getting scared and wasn't sure what to do next. Well, this is part of what's getting me down. Why am I so damned dumb? I hear the other guys . . . I mean, like everything's real cool . . . they're always talking about "making out" with their dates . . . they seem to know their way around. Wonder if some of it is big talk? I know I talk big sometimes, and I'm always afraid some of the gang will find out I can't back it up.

I wish I had other guys' confidence in themselves. Hell, I never feel as if I'm measuring up. I wish I'd been born a different person who didn't have feelings like this. And when I'm down I chop people off real short. Gad, I hate myself sometimes . . . and everybody else too . . . they seem so much better than I am . . . it's hard not to be jealous. People keep telling me that I'm better than I think I am, but I can't seem to believe it. The more they expect of me the worse I do. I wish I wouldn't pay any attention to them and what they expect. When I took that exam today the thought of everybody's expectations made me forget what I knew. Gee, I really like to study and find out about things and me, but I want to do it my way.

Ah, here's Mom now. Hi, Mom. There's Mary. Let's get going . . . I'm late. . . . Where have you been?

. . . . .

> *Jake*—Jerry's friend. Jerry and Jake have just spent an hour and a half working on a chemistry assignment and Jerry has returned home. Jake is lying on his bed.

God, I'm tired. I never feel like doing anything. I'm not getting my homework done. . . . I haven't shoveled the snow off the walks yet . . . Dad'll raise hell. But so what? He's already decided I'm no good anyhow so there's no point in trying.

I get sore as hell when some adult starts talking about teen-agers as a kind of animal. They say, "Teen-agers are . . ." (it doesn't matter what they say—it's always bad news). My Dad says, "punk kid" all the time about what teen-agers do. . . . It's as if he was indirectly talking about me, or about what he's afraid I'll turn out to be.

Jerry makes me mad . . . he works at things and keeps trying. He seems to be reaching for something, but I'm afraid to. I want to stay where I am, but I'd sure as heck like to be free. Somebody's always breathing down my neck. I wish I belonged to another family, like Jerry's.

You can tell Jerry's Dad likes him and has confidence in him. And his mother's great, and nice looking considering how old she is. She doesn't nag him all the time. Ma's too busy, and she never listens. . . . Dad's always working in his shop or at some meeting. Both of them are always pushing me . . . they say I'll never amount to anything unless I get going. But I don't want to go anywhere . . . I just want to stay here . . . but I wish things were different.

.   .   .   .   .

Jake—on Sunday

That did it! When Dad and Ma said that I ought to go to church, that it would be good for me and make me behave, I hit the roof. I'm sick of being told what I ought to do. Sometimes when I'm in church I can hardly breathe. . . . I mean, I want to rush out of there to where I can breathe again, and fling my arms, and run and shout, and be free.

Now they've taken away a part of my allowance. God, I hate them! . . . I wish they'd drop dead.

.   .   .   .   .

Mary—Jerry's sister

I wish I knew who I am. I sometimes look in the mirror and wonder, what is me? I'm not always the same . . . with adults I'm different than I am with my own crowd . . . and then I'm still something else inside me (privately) . . . are these all the same me? There are times when I'm afraid that no one of these selves is really me . . . then I'm afraid I'll never find out who I am.

Another thing, I hate myself when I try to be the kind of person somebody else wants me to be. This is why I fight with Mom . . . she wants me to be a lady and she has ideas about what kind of person a lady is. She's so old-fashioned it's a pain! My world's different than hers . . . I can't be her kind of lady. I'd rather be me than a lady, anyhow. But why can't I be both, that is, be me?

Daddy likes me the way I am . . . he's a doll, the greatest . . . we understand each other. He does worry about Bill and me, though. I feel sorry for him. Sometimes he looks real sad as if he's missing something. . . . I wish I could do something for him. It's sure wonderful to have him think I'm someone real special.

Being me is terribly complicated. And it's getting more complicated. I feel so different than I used to. I notice it most when I'm with Bill. He thinks I'm special, the most. Wonder if he really loves me . . . he says he does. Anyhow, he makes being me being a girl. Always before I was just a person, and now I'm a *girl* person. Being a girl has become something special . . . but it's both wonderful and scary. I guess I'm becoming a woman . . . I feel a lot more than I can say. Sometimes when I'm with Bill I feel a lot more than I can express and then at other times I can't talk at all. This worries him. I mean, everything seems a lot simpler for him. He studies, plays football, and dates me. And on dates he either wants to do something like going to the movies or he wants to pet. Things aren't that simple for me. Sometimes I feel real close to him and happy, and sometimes I'm irritable and I don't want him to touch me. Sometimes I know I love him and then at other times I'm not so sure. I mean, I don't understand myself. No wonder he doesn't know what to make of me sometimes. I don't know whether or not I want to get married. Sometimes I think I'd like to have a career, do something important and be famous. But that's silly! I'm nobody and I couldn't do anything important. Yet I'd hate to get married only because I couldn't do anything else . . . maybe I won't even get married because nobody will want me. I think Mother's afraid I'll be an old maid . . . she keeps pushing me at the boys.

·   ·   ·   ·   ·

Bill—getting ready for a date with Mary

It's hard to believe that I'm almost through high school. Wonder what I'll be doing this time next year. I ought to be hearing from U pretty soon . . . sure hope they take me. Hope Dad won't be too disappointed . . . He wanted me to go to his school. He was a big name there but I want to make my own way. He was great when I told him I'd sent my application to U . . . I can tell he really hopes they'll take me.

He's had some tough breaks. Mother's death last year and then failing to be made general manager as he had expected. He's got guts. When Mother died I remember his saying, "The important thing is not what happens to a man but what he does about what happens to him." You can count on Dad . . . he practices what he preaches. That's what he did when I got in trouble with the police two years ago because of careless driving. He was mad but all he said was, "O.K., it's happened. You know why and you know the price you have to pay . . . now what are you going to do about it?" Gad, he sure did believe in me, and I guess that's why I believe in myself. Sure is funny how one's moods vary, though. Sometimes I'm high, as now, and I feel as if I could do anything . . . other times when I'm way down I don't feel as if I can do anything. Thank God I'm mostly up now. There's so much to live for and do. . . . I want to go to school . . . I also want to see the world and work at different kinds of jobs before I make up my mind. This is a great time to be alive. I like living in the space age with all the new things there are to learn and do.

I feel strong and would like to get at things. I remember when I didn't feel this way. When I was scrawny and scared I was ashamed of myself, my body, the way I felt about things, and I was always dropping things and breaking them. . . . I couldn't trust myself and I didn't think anybody liked me. I sure felt like a mess. Now it's different. I had a lot of help from Dad . . . his confidence in me never wavered . . . from Mother, too, before she died . . . and old Mr. Jim, the math teacher, who taught me to think . . . and Purdy, the coach. They talked with me about things and made me think them through. These people all stood for something . . . just the thought of them gives me something to think about and live for.

Lately I've begun to think that I can be a part of something tremendous and much bigger than any of us. I want to be a part of it. . . . It's like being a part of a team . . . behind the scenes but very much a part of it. Someone like the coach . . . like in a game . . . I want to throw myself into it not caring what happens as long as we play well, and yet wanting to win. . . . But what is winning in this new game that I seem to be joining? Our minister thinks I'm discovering the religious dimension of my life. Maybe . . . I can't follow the church's ideas, but if there's something there I'd like to find it. It's as if some part of me is going to join up with another part of me. I sense an excitement growing within me that makes it impossible to "play it cool." I don't want to keep things "cool" . . . yet I notice that people often look at me in a certain way if I show enthusiasm. The other day one of the guys said, "Down, Bill, down, or you'll get noticed and get in trouble." Is it possible the system of society is out to keep me and others from getting excited about things and going all out for them?

I wonder if Mary will be ready. She's a keen gal. I hope she's in a good mood and ready for some fun. I'll bet I could talk to her about these things. When I get angry with her and tell her what's on my mind, even if I hurt her, we then often understand each other better. Then she does the same thing, and that helps us too.

why this book

"I get sore as hell when some adult starts talking about teen-agers as a kind of animal. They say, "Teen-agers are ..." ("it doesn't matter what they say—it's always bad news). My Dad says, "punk kid" all the time about what teen-agers do. . . . It's as if he was indirectly talking about me, or about what he's afraid I'll turn out to be."—*Jake*

When Jerry and Mary and Jake and Bill were babies, each of them seemed to themselves to be the center of everything because so many people acted toward them as if they were the center. And so it was with you and all of us. When you cried someone usually came running to help you; when you were hungry you were fed; when wet, you were changed; people and their activities seemed to center in you and your needs. After a while you began to take this for granted. You even developed a belief that you were the center of all life. Gradually, however, this condition changed. You learned to eat when others ate, to act for yourselves in place of crying for help, to go to the bathroom by yourselves, to be aware of other persons' needs and to learn to help them. This change meant that you had to change your belief. You are not the center of everything; the world does not exist to cater to your needs and whims.

Thoughtful men through the centuries have found their center outside of themselves, in the service of love, of truth, of justice, in God, although today the Word of God has lost its meaning for many people because men have allowed small, mean, and hostile concepts of God to hide the One Who is the source and sustainer of life. But my point is that we know the center of our life cannot be in ourselves but in something big outside that makes us grow and keeps us humble.

Such a painful change in your attitudes and expectations required change in your behavior. No longer could you express your love or rage or fear without restraint. And yet your feelings and moods as young persons are just as strong as they ever were. You have had to keep them under some control. You have had to become aware of other "I's," you have had to learn to surrender your desires for other purposes, and you have had to learn to postpone satisfactions to some future time. And you have also begun to see that your own well-being is dependent on that of others, and that you all get along better when you are concentrating on something bigger than yourselves. Bill, you remember, was beginning to experience that conviction. In football he had learned that the game was more important than the individual concerns and jealousies of the team members. He was also beginning to sense a more profound meaning of life than any he had known before. Jerry and Mary are still feeling the pull between childhood's concern for self and those larger concerns that are now calling to them. Jake, though, is still a self-centered and frustrated boy who is afraid of all that lies ahead.

As we read the soliloquies of Jerry and Mary and Jake and Bill we realize how much of what they say is in response to the people with whom they live. Our environment is important, and our personal environment is most important of all. The attitudes and expectations of the people with whom we live influence our concept of ourselves and our capacities. People who make us feel inadequate cause moods of discouragement and depression. Jake, for example, thinks of himself as a failure and is depressed because that is how his parents see him. On the other hand, people who characteristically believe in us awaken our confidence in ourselves so that our mood level is higher. Bill is a good illustration of such a cause and effect. With some people we feel freer and more responsible; others make us afraid and rebellious.

One of the most difficult things about being a young person between the ages of fourteen and twenty is the feeling and opinion that people have about you. It is almost impossible for them to see you as you are. They associate all sorts of things with you. All the terms used to describe you—"adolescent," "teen-ager"—conjure up images that imprison you. You are thought of as being in what is called a "problem stage" of life. You are thought of as an animal, even referred to as such, remembering Jake's explosive comment. Because you are neither child nor adult, you are regarded as being in "limbo." You are thought to be in protest against everyone and, therefore, are feared because if you had your own way you would upset everybody's apple cart. By some you are supposed to be a seething caldron of sexual interest and passion because of recently erupted sexual drives. Another prevailing image of you is that of reckless drivers who are threats to the safety of others on the highways. You are also regarded as creatures of unpredictable moods. You are seen as restless, always on the go, and filled with so many of these unpredictable moods that it is almost impossible for others to live with you.

Behind these and all other images people have of you

there are the real persons that you are now and are becoming. There are other and more positive things that can be said about you if images have not driven you into extremes of rebellion that hide what you really are. What are they? You see things clearly, so clearly that you often embarrass adults with your lucidity. You are also capable of an honesty that frightens adults. You are idealistic in the sense that you believe in such things as justice, equality, loyalty, fidelity. You are quite capable of getting caught up in causes, looking for opportunities for service to others. The Peace Corps, for example, has a tremendous appeal for you. You hate compromise and would like to let the chips fall where they will. You are interested in relationships and are troubled when people do not get along well together, and you would like to be able in some way to mend human relationships. You want to try new ways of doing things, and you are avidly interested in the person that you are and are about to be.

Adolescence is a time of change and, therefore, a time of disturbance and conflict. In the course of this transition you have many experiences which produce in you a variety of responses. Some of these responses are moods that are emotionally reinforced states of mind or attitudes. Moods can be very strong and may hold an individual captive for either a short or long time. Your moods are an important part of your life and can be both helpful and destructive. They are important to you because they represent both meaning and energy. A mood of depression causes you to think and feel despondently as if there is no purpose or hope in anything, and such a mood drains your energy so that you feel empty and passive. A mood of elation, on the other hand, produces in you happy, excited feelings that anticipate good experiences you might have. At these times your level of energy is high, so high in fact that it may be hard for you to sit still.

I am writing this book because it is my belief that the meanings and energies of these moods can be used in creative ways. Even the sad and depressed ones can be useful. It is not necessary for us to be helpless in the grip of our moods. Rather, may we hope to be able to recognize them and direct their meaning and energy toward constructive ends.

This view of moods is important not only to young people but to parents, teachers, and others who are responsible for youth. And so I write for them too. Some of the tragedy of human relationships stems from the misunderstanding that exists between young people and adults and from a common lack of understanding about the nature of moods. Both should realize that adults have moods, too. Although adults learn to control them as they grow older, they unfortunately forget their moods when they were strongest in their youth. When adults encounter these moods in young people, their own anxieties, despairs, and enthusiasms are dimly reactivated, which causes them to view adolescents and their moods with alarm. But their fear is as much a product of their own experiences as of the teen-agers'.

I am suggesting that you need to know that an adult's response to you is often defensive. Many of you are disillusioned by this realization. You feel it is unjust for parents to be so needy and defensive. But you need to shed your illusions about parents and all other people. Disillusionment is a necessary result of education and growing up because illusions need to be replaced by understandings that are real. You should try to remember that your bitterness over the failures and betrayals of adults and the

injustices of the culture into which you were born un-
nerves many grown-ups. Your idealism and unwillingness
to compromise make disillusioned and compromising adults
uncomfortable whose living is a search for security by way
of conformity.

Two sets of people, teachers and ministers, who ought
to wield tremendous influence on you, are often your be-
trayers because they value content and tradition more than
persons. You are often disappointed in your mentors because they seem unable to accept you as you are and to
travel with you as you move into maturity. Instead of being
understanding and helpful they seem more concerned about
the organizations, institutions, and systems which they represent. As a result, they expect you to conform rather than
help you find your own creative relation to things as they
are. On the other hand, you should not expect life to meet
you freely and perfectly. Your encounters with leaders who
do not lead, and guides who have sold their souls for security and comfort, can become a part of your education
for a life and a world that contains just these kinds of
people. The risk in this is that you might become like
them. One of the greatest things that you should fear is
the loss of your creativity.

This brings me to the second reason for writing this
book. I am saddened by the evident loss of creativity in
the living of a great many people. All of us should seek
ways of preserving or restoring and further cultivating creative possibilities of others. These powers are all too com-
monly lost. It is obvious that children have them; it is to
be seen in their joy and spontaneity, their eagerness to
improvise; their imaginative powers that enable them to
make the commonest things into the most wonderful; their
capacity to love and to give; their readiness to laugh and

weep; their sense of a world beyond the world they see. These capacities are too wonderful to be lost. Some adults justify their loss of these capacities by saying they are not practical and have no place in the work-a-day world. After their creative phase, children move into the latency period and their creative capacities begin to disappear. During the process children often become more and more defensive, rigid, and conformist as they slip into an unimaginative and conventional-minded adult life. Even as they learn to talk and shape their concepts they are learning to stifle rather than direct their impulses, and repress rather than express their meanings because of moralistic and conformist pressures exerted by teachers, and their own peer treatment of each other.

The initial loss in the power of creativity seems to occur in the time of pre-adolescence. Since adolescence is recognized as a time of second chance at life because of the changes that take place in the person, why could it not also be a time of rediscovery and renewal. Because of these physiological, psychological, and sociological changes and the new personal resources that the individual is acquiring, the creative potentialities of the individual ought to be heightened and furthered. My hope is that if these powers have been smothered in you, the reading and studying of this book may help them to be released so that you may finally possess your birthright as a creative person.

Being creative is a way of being religious. I believe that the Creator God wants us to be creative. He wants us to find the new and deeper meanings of life; to daringly seek to live with each other cooperatively. Unfortunately, too much religious emphasis has been on being "good" in a very narrow sense. Most of the Sunday schools you attended could not accept your natural behavior, your doubts and questions. They stressed good behavior which meant conformity to the way some adults thought you should act. As a result too many of you feel that God will not love you if you are not "good." For this reason you may think of church and religion as being repressive and against the things that are most important to you. Actually, the goodness God wants of us is best expressed through an honest concern for others and the conditions in which they have to live. The truly good are the courageous people who spend their lives serving something or someone else. It takes courage not to sell out all values for the sake of yourself. According to the teaching of Jesus the "smart guy" is the one who invests himself in something beyond himself. Then if he does wrong or sins and is sorry, he is provided forgiveness which leaves him free to be courageous and creative. This is what the good news of the gospel is.

If your creative powers have not been smothered, then I hope the thoughts contained here will give you courage to persist in your exploration, study, thinking, feeling, and your deciding and acting, so that you will become more and more the person who will meet life on the frontiers of its meaning for you. I shall undertake to do this in the next chaper by identifying what moods are and what they do to you; in the following chapters by examining the causes of your moods and by studying the power of purposes over your moods; and in the last two chapters by discussing some of the resources you may employ in dealing with moods.

moods and what they do to you

"The whole deal gets me down . . . when I'm like this I can't talk to anybody. . . . I wish I had other guys' confidence in themselves. I never feel as if I'm measuring up. . . . When I'm down I chop people off real short. Gad, I hate myself sometimes . . . and everybody else. . . . Sure, he [Dad] loves me, but I sure as hell wish he would get off my back once in a while."—*Jerry*

"God, I'm tired. I never feel like doing anything. I'm not getting my homework done. . . . I haven't shoveled the snow off the walks yet. . . . Dad'll raise hell, but so what? He's already decided I'm no good anyhow. . . . Now they've [parents] taken away part of my allowance. God, I hate them! . . . I wish they'd drop dead."—*Jake*

"Sure is funny how one's moods vary . . . sometimes I'm high, as now, and I feel as if I could do anything . . . other times when I'm down I don't feel as if I can do anything. Thank God I'm mostly up now. There's so much to live for and do."—*Bill*

I have already referred to moods as conscious states of mind and strong feelings which may hold you captive for either a short or long time, and which can be either helpful or destructive to you. We all have moods; some of us more than others. There are some people who are very moody and are more completely the victims of their moods. This is true of Jake whose mood level is low most of the time. Jerry and his sister are up and down, whereas Bill seems

32

to have come through with moods that are predominantly high.

What are some of the varieties of moods that you find in yourselves?

Moods provide a part of the atmosphere in which you live. You have your anxieties about yourselves and others that account for many of your moods. If your grades are not as good as those of others or your social life is not as active, you are apt to be discouraged, depressed, and self-depreciating. If you excel and do better than others you are reassured, become elated and full of vigor and confidence. You may then be tempted to rejoice when other people do not do as well in order that you may seem to do better, with the result that you may be overcome by the mood of guilt.

Most of you at one time or another run the gamut between the height of elation and the depths of despair. You may move from quickly rising enthusiasms that tend to sweep you and others off your feet to times of utter hopelessness when life seems to be a "bum deal." As Jerry said, "the whole thing seems like a trap. I'm stuck with all these problems . . . I didn't ask to be born. The whole deal gets me down."

Another characteristic of your moods is to be found in your burning, and at other times, sterile, intellectual and philosophical preoccupations. Adolescence is a time when you begin to be able to use concepts and think philosophically. The world of ideas beckons to you, and it is fun to use these new-found powers. But you can get lost in the intricacies of your thought, become frightened by the questions that seem to have no answer, and bewildered by the unfaithfulness and compromise that you see in the living and thinking of others.

Other moods are born out of your yearning for freedom, by your rebellions against structure and form. You find it necessary to test the teaching and disciplines of home, school, and church to see if they have validity. The authority of others must be challenged in order that you may grow your own sense of authority which is essential to being a person. The demands of convention and standards of behavior often seem like obstacles to you who are in the process of becoming. Out of these encounters, these questionings and challenges come moods of rebellion and anger and frustration, as when Jerry said that he wished his Dad would get off his back.

Closely related to them is a sense of loneliness which you experience because the world you have to live in has been made by someone else, and you have not yet found or made your own world. Furthermore, having only recently acquired your abilities for understanding and relating you are often insecure in your new relationships with everybody, and the old ones that served your childhood are no longer adequate.

You also experience feelings of being oppressed by your parents. You get the impression that your parents do not think you can do anything important by yourselves, and that when you do undertake something it will not be good enough to please them. They always seem to be "griping" about things, and you may develop feelings of despair about getting along with them or about ever being rid of them.

Then there are the moods that grow out of your impotent rages and active hates which are often directed against the adult world that sometimes seems invincibly organized against you. This was Jake's feeling when he said, "Now they [referring to his parents] have taken away a part of my allowance. God, I hate them! . . . I wish they'd drop dead." Some of his feeling is directed toward the policies and representatives of organized society, most of whom seem to have it in for teen-agers.

Then there are the moods that result from your erotic feelings. Your crushes on male or female can either be homosexually or heterosexually directed. They come and go and produce in you moods of elation or of despondency; your longings for intimacy and your fear of it; your sense of sexual power, and your need for physical contact coupled with your awareness of the mystery that it represents. Jerry experienced this in his relationship with Janie. Sometimes you love your bodies and sometimes you hate them. You may suffer from a foreboding disquiet because so many conflicting things are being said about sex that confuse your thinking about all the wonderful and frightening feelings that you have in response to it.

Sometimes you may be attacked by feelings of utter worthlessness when it seems as if you are wholly inadequate, and you even think of ways of escaping your miserable existence. And yet any suicidal fantasies that you may have often include the thought about how sorry people will be when they discover that you are dead! Your sense of inferiority demands an answer, and sometimes the answer seems to be the elimination of yourself in some way. Fortunately, your longing for life and the thrust of your energy soon moves you out of the shadows and back in the warmth of friends and the promise of love.

Such are some of your moods. Now the question is: What do they do to you?

Thus far we have seen that moods have power over you, and we should now examine their power.

We have also observed that some moods tear you down and others build you up. Moods have power, whether negative or positive, because they represent both *meaning* and *energy*. The *energy* aspect of moods is easily identified because it either adds to or takes away from your general and normal supply of vitality and pep. One teen-ager, after asking whether negative moods really hinder our achievement, decided that they did. He said, "They cause you to get bogged down. They make you feel that you don't want to do anything but sit around and mope and feel sorry for yourself." The *meaning* of a mood is identified in its content. The content of a depressive mood is "how bad things are," and the content of a mood of elation is love, hope, happiness, and confidence.

Moods affect three areas of your lives: 1. your relationships with others; 2. your supply of energy for the business of life; 3. your capacity to deal with the issues of life.

First, moods affect your relationships with others. We have already noted that these relationships are important; that with some people you feel freer and more responsible, and other people, on the contrary, make you more afraid and rebellious. You tend to measure up to other peoples' attitudes toward and expectations of you. If your important people act toward you as if you are intelligent and capable, then this becomes your image of yourself. If, in contrast, people view you as being clumsy and inept, then you are very apt to *be* clumsy and inept. Jake, for instance, obviously acquired his low opinion of himself from his father who, according to Jake, has decided that Jake's "no good anyhow." Bill's self-respect seems to have come from the respect he received from his father.

While you are influenced by other people's view of you, you must not allow yourself to be limited by their opinions of you. Equally binding, sometimes, are people's good opinions of you. One young person said that she resented being told that she was a good girl and could be counted on always to do the right thing. You do have freedom to rise above the opinions and expectations of others.

Another aspect of your relationship with people is your influence on them. Human relationships are mutual, that is, two-way. You need people and they need you.

Love calls forth love, but love has to be expressed in ways that can be understood by the one who is being loved. Love has to be given in relation to need: the need to be loved and the need to love. Relationships are not that simple, however. Fear is experienced in relation to love because human love meets only some of your needs and disappoints you, too. Early in your lives you learn fear in relation to love. You feared that mother and others would not respond to your needs and that you would be frustrated if not met. You learned both to have a fear of her and to fear for yourselves. When the need for love and the need to love are frustrated by fear, resentment comes. This is why it is true that you can hate and hurt those whom you love and who love you. You resent being "disappointed in love" and being made afraid.

The condition just described causes many of your moods, especially the ones that make you act against others and alienate you from them. Resentment and hostility, for example, cause you to draw yourselves in protectingly and turn aggressively against others as if they were your enemies. Your guilty moods often cause you to make other people scapegoats for your own guilt, criticizing them instead of seeing and accepting your own responsibility for what is wrong. It is as if you can now accept yourselves because you have successfully, justifiably criticized others. The first tragic effect of these moods is that you become separated from one another; and the second tragic result of such moods is that their effect makes you more guilty, more hostile, more resentful.

There is a prevailing belief that if you are hostile, you should express your hostility; that in expressing it, you will get rid of it. Nothing could be more untrue. You only succeed in establishing patterns for the expression of resentments which the inevitable and endless frustrations of life continue to produce. "If this is true," asks a teen-ager, "what are you supposed to do with your hostility?"

If you can remember that your hostility is related to your love as the two sides of a coin are related, you may be better able to do something other than explode your resentments. You may be able to explode with less venom; you may be able to do something constructive such as trying to understand the person whom you resent, or understand why you are as angry as you are.

On the other hand, there are the more positive moods of acceptance and love which, when expressed adequately, tend to break down the barriers of separation and alienation, and bind you more closely together. These are what you may call benign moods, moods of good will, of affirmation. One reason why these moods are not more effective is that you are not as apt to express them as you are the negative ones. There are times when you say of yourselves, "Oh, I'm in a good mood." There are some natural expressions of such moods. You may whistle or sing, you may carry yourselves in a cheerful, jaunty way; your tone of voice may have a lilt in it, and you may treat people with good humor, in a spirit of tolerance and forgiveness. It is a case of feeling so good that you can afford to be kind.

These positive moods may be strengthened by responding to them. You may say, for example, "I feel like writing to so-and-so and tell her how much she has meant to me."

Too often you do not act on these thoughts with the result that the mood passes and you do not get the permanent benefit of it. You do not build it into your character through appropriate action.

An important part of your relationship with other people is your communiciation with them. Moods affect your communication for good or ill. Remember that Jerry admitted that when he was "down I chop people off real short . . . I hate myself sometimes . . . and everybody else." When some moods grip you, you cannot talk or act (action is non-verbal communication, and no talking is action and says something for you and about you). If you do not or cannot communicate, then your relationship will suffer and go from bad to worse. Jerry observed that his sister, when in certain kinds of moods, would not say anything for days. In this connection he observed that "she looks as if she is thinking unhappy things." Sometimes your communication becomes so inhibited that your relationships break down.[1]

Other moods make communication easier and freer. When you are happy and confident, living in response to people you like and who seem to like you, you acquire a freedom and eloquence of communication that is above your usual level and quite exciting. Such communication usually nurtures relationships so that you grow to trust each other more, and are able to assume more responsibility for one another. Mary and Bill were experiencing some of this enabling effect of moods born of love and confidence.

Second, your moods affect your supply of energy for the business of living. They either generate or diminish energy. Energy output changes as rapidly as your moods. You can move with lightning speed from peppy spontaneity to

[1] See chapter on Resources for dealing with moods.

lethargic hopelessness, and in a twinkling of an eye you can move from the depths to the heights. One day Mary was moping around the house despondent because, for the moment, she did not think anybody liked her. Her mother tried to get her to call up some of her friends and make plans to do something, but she was too tired to move. Later in the afternoon the phone rang. A friend was calling to tell her about a conversation she had overheard in which a very real compliment had been paid to Mary. Her voice changed, and when the conversation was over she danced and sang about the house and on her own initiative called up a couple of her friends to go skating.

Moods of indecision and inadequacy sap your energies. "God, I'm tired," said Jake, "I never feel like doing anything. I'm not getting my homework done. . . . I haven't shoveled the snow off the walks yet. . . . Dad'll raise hell." Lack of purpose in living, uncertainties about issues, the absence of anything to commit yourself to also depress and fatigue you. It is important, therefore, that you who are passionate people with a great deal to give and a need to give should find ways to give that both release and cultivate your creativity.

Third, moods affect your capacity to deal with the issues of life. All too often your moods confuse the issue. For example, you may substitute rebellions for more constructive purposes. Rebellion for rebellion's sake accomplishes nothing, but rebellion against real enemies such as ignorance and dishonesty is rebellion put to good use.

Young people face real issues today. What are you going to do with your lives, something or nothing? Are you going to take on the wreckage you have inherited and the resources that come to you from the past, or is your revolt going to be a repudiation of everything? Do you have the courage to work out your own sexual identity and responsibility without too much dependence on the taboos of an earlier time or without discarding past values altogether? Are you going to accept the challenges to work out ways of life that are appropriate to your own times and circumstances, or will you succumb to the moods of blind acceptance of the dictates of others and an imposition upon yourself and others regardless?

You live in a time when ancient ways and institutions seem to be crumbling, and sometimes it seems as if you have nothing certain on which to build for the future. And yet you do have some sense of the strength that comes to you from the past and you look back to it with some longing. At the same time you feel a vision and pull of the future. You have a sense of its possibilities and are moved by the challenge of the need to work out new forms and to realize new truths. You thus are caught in a bind between the past and the future. The bind is made worse because the adult, whose world is faltering and whose institutions are crumbling, out of his own panic often brings pressure upon you to conform to what has been, and will never be again. To conform would mean the death not only of the new generation but of their own unborn culture. Faithfulness to yourselves and to your own day sometimes requires unfaithfulness to and rebellion against that which has been, except insofar as enduring truth from the past can be built into the future. Jesus himself rebelled against some of the teaching of his elders, but he also embodied its best meanings. It is inevitable and desirable that in the course of the process you will become critical of things as they are. The meaning and energy of your critical moods must be translated into constructive action. But you must be equally responsive to the possibilities of new thoughts and ways of acting, and for commitment to them. The meaning and energy of your moods will find creative expression in courageous action.

We older people need your anger at our hyprocrisy, your prophetic discontent with the way things are, your search for the meaning of life that we missed, and your impatience to find a way to serve. We need these from you even though we may defensively rebel against them; we need them to keep all that we fought for in our times from being lost.

The worldwide revolutions in the areas of race and nationalism, in technological and urban development, in relationships between nations and the new ways they need to develop for settling differences, confront you and all emerging adults with so many questions and possibilities that they challenge both your courage and your creativity. Contemporary life inevitably affects your mood life and the mood life of all young people throughout the world. Your go-go-go attitude can be harnessed for creative action or it can drive you to flight from the challenges. It is not only your decision but the decision of all young people throughout the world. In responding to the challenges of our own time we are responding to God. We believe that this is true because we also believe that he acts through people as they face the issues of life. The asking of a responsible honest question may be a service not only to man but to God. Thus the expression of the meaning and energy of a positive or negative mood may serve a religious purpose. And in so doing we can be following our Lord's example.

what causes moods

"He's sure a big jerk . . . seems so sure of himself. . . . I wish I could put some beef on my bones so I'd feel like a man. I wish I could've made that long run last Saturday in the game with Cedar High instead of Bill. Then they'd have cheered me instead of him. Me? What can I do? Dad says, though, that my day will come.

He's a great guy but he's too darned successful for me. Who wants to live the way he does! . . . I wonder if he's ever had my kind of problems. . . . I mean, he couldn't have or he wouldn't be where he is. . . . Sure, he loves me, but I sure as hell wish he'd get off my back once in a while. Why should I let him live my life, too.

Sometimes I like the idea of growing up . . . then again I'm not so sure. Things are getting tougher . . . and everybody's always yelling about grades . . . teachers, parents, and even a lot of kids always pushing for top grades. I'd like to try different things but I'm afraid I'll fail. . . . When I took that exam today the thought of everybody's expectations made me forget what I knew.

At first Mary wouldn't say . . . then she bawled again and said she was so ugly that no boy would ever marry her what with her teeth and complexion."—*Jerry*

"This is why I fight with Mom. She wants me to be a lady and she has ideas about what kind of person a lady is. She's

so old-fashioned it's a pain! My world's different than her's
. . . I can't be her kind of lady. I'd rather be me than a lady,
anyhow. But why can't I be both, that is, be me?"—*Mary*

"I feel strong and would like to get at things. I remember
when I didn't feel this way. When I was scrawny and scared
I was ashamed of myself, my body, the way I felt about
things, and I was always dropping things and breaking them.
. . . I couldn't trust myself and I didn't think anybody liked
me. I sure felt like a mess. Now it's different. I had a lot of
help from Dad . . . his confidence in me never wavered . . .
from Mother, too, before she died . . and old Mr. Jim, the
math teacher, who taught me to think . . . and Purdy, the coach.
These people all stood for something . . . just the thought of them
gives me something to think about and live for."—*Bill*

Moods are produced by conditions both within and outside you. They are the signs of stress and strain, symptoms
of uncertainty and conflict. You, the people around you,
and the circumstances of your life, all contribute to the
occurrence of your moods. Let us look at each of these in
turn, though remembering that they do not exist independently of each other.

A. There are, first, the forces inside you.

Changes take place in you during your teens that make
you a different person. Not only does your size and shape
change, but forces develop and are released in you that
cause you to cease to be a child with a child's needs and
capacities and move you toward adulthood. Unfortunately,
however, the transition from childhood to adulthood takes
quite a few years, and this period of transition becomes
confusing for both you and those who are responsible for
and to you. As society becomes more complex the period
between biological maturity and adulthood becomes wider,
causes frustrations, and breeds moods. Your physiological
and anatomical changes are exciting but are also confusing

and necessitate a change in your relationships with boys and girls and men and women. The patterns you have used up to this time are no longer adequate for the requirements of your lives, and you are under the necessity of finding new ones which are not readily acquired.

Because of these changes you are faced with three tasks during your adolescence. First, you have the task of liberating yourselves from your old attachments and of achieving self-reliance and self-direction. Second, you face the task of completing your sexual development and becoming heterosexual adults whose primary interest is in the opposite sex. And third, you have the task of deciding what you are going to do with your lives, including the choice, if you have a choice, of how you will make a living. This last task includes choosing who and what you will serve: Who will your God be, and how you will serve him or it.

These changes, and the tasks they impose, are all producers of moods. We see the evidence of these effects in the soliloquies of Jerry and Jake and Mary and Bill. Mary is obviously wrestling with the changes taking place in her, and because of them sometimes she is happy and other times sad. We may be sure that often she is not sure what causes her moods, though as she matures she will gather more and more insight about their cause and, therefore, achieve more and more independence in relation to them. Jake is not making much progress with his development. He is still in a state of childish rebellion against his parents which tends to keep him immature and prevents him from being able to face the tasks that his development requires of him. Jerry is in the midst of his struggle, partly living out his old patterns of relationship with his father and mother and others, and partly struggling with his new concepts of himself and his new roles. Sometimes he is in a state of rebellion against the old patterns; sometimes he is frightened by the new; sometimes he is caught in the bind between the two. All these kinds of relationships produce the various moods which he suffers or enjoys. Bill, on the other hand, is farther advanced than the others. He has more fully completed his tasks and with some real success. His moods, therefore, are more under his control than they were earlier when he refers to times when he was the victim of them. He is acquiring a sense of God and of his own relation to Him. He thinks of being a part of something tremendous and much bigger than any of us. "I want to be a part of it." Having been given a concept of God, Bill is now beginning to formulate the meaning of his own experience of God.

We might think of these tasks as the work of youth. As children you all depended upon your parents and teachers. By their acceptance of you, you were better able to accept yourselves. Their love for you gave you the experience of being loved even when you were unlovable, so that you learned to love yourselves and could begin to grow and have the power to love others. Your experience of being loved also provided the basis for understanding the nature of love, and the meaning of the belief that God is love. When we experience love, regardless of whether we have earned or are worthy of it, we are learning through human means that this is true love and true of God's love. We can further believe that in loving others we are also expressing God's love for them. Your experience of love also awakened in you the awareness of yourselves as persons, made you free to be your own separate person. But the time came when it was necessary for you to withdraw from the first form of parental love because it had outlived its usefulness.

The gradual withdrawal from this first relationship for the sake of self-awareness is a crucial moment in the history of all of you. At some time during your adolescence you need to withdraw from the close, intimate, and confidential relationship you had as children. You need to be alone. Your thoughts are not as open as they used to be. You need to repudiate parental standards, tastes, ideas, faiths, and ways of doing as a part of the process of achieving your own which will build on and reaffirm some of the things you had thrown out. You need to rebel against parental supervision and interference as you achieve your own sense of authority. You are apt to become secretive and morose, preoccupied and thoughtful. These and all the other characteristics that we might name are signs that you are trying to disentangle that which is yourselves from all that is not yourselves. To accomplish this you must go apart for a while and withdraw into yourselves. You must isolate yourselves momentarily in order to examine the results of having lived in relationship. Sometimes it is in radical loneliness that you will find yourselves. In the midst of this withdrawal and loneliness you will experience all kinds of moods.

There is one positive side to this experience. The withdrawal from relationship, as a part of the process of finding yourselves, is a necessary part of the work of youth in order that you may be able to reenter relationships more responsibly as a person who knows who he is in his own right and with some possession of his own uniqueness and powers.

Withdrawal from a dependent parental relationship is an occasion for the movement in you toward a reaching for God. Because of your finiteness you must always be dependent upon someone, even while you acquire independence and learn to assume responsibility for your own life. During adolescence you begin to sense, as did Bill, a "presence" beyond us, a need for relation with someone who completes our being and heals the brokenness that we both cause and suffer. Out of the loss of childhood's relationships and the resulting loneliness may come a new sense of ourselves, of others, and of God.

During this time many fears and anxieties are experienced. Your withdrawals are often frightening. You are afraid because you often feel very much alone. You are often afraid of giving up the dependencies of childhood, and yet you know you cannot keep them. You can also be afraid of the responsibilities that will come with maturity, and yet you also want those responsibilities. You can even be afraid because you seem so confused and ambivalent about these contradictions. And you can be afraid because people seem so different than they used to. You can be afraid in the midst of achieving your new relationships with your peers of both sexes as, for instance, when Jerry was glad when Janie stopped their petting because he was getting scared and was not sure what to do next.

During this time also you experience conflicts between your desire to protect yourselves and to express yourselves. You seek to protect yourselves from the demands of others, the grueling demands, to assume responsibility to produce, to take initiative in ordering your lives, to meet complex situations in society and in your relationships with others.

And yet with all this there is the desire within yourselves to be creative, to express yourselves, to take the initiative, to think, decide, and act on your own, to throw off as much as possible your dependencies upon others. You want both to be invisible and also to stand up prominently and be counted. Bill wrestled with this problem and reached the point in his life where he participated in his living with real enthusiasm and expectation, and yet some of his friends thought that this was a dangerous thing for him to do. One of them remarked, "Down, Bill, down, or you'll get noticed and in trouble."

As you face the possibility of more responsibility you experience a fear that is well known to all of us, the fear of failure. Jerry said of himself, "I'd like to try different things but I'm afraid I'll fail." Many of you dream of doing important and creative things but you are sometimes kept from doing them for fear that your efforts will not be successful. All of us have to learn to take a chance. To be successful means that you will have to risk the possibility of failure; and if you will not risk failure, you cannot possibly achieve success. Actually, you have nothing to lose, especially when you remember that you can learn from failures. They can become steps on the way to creative expression and accomplishment. But the fear of failure produces many of the moods that you experience.

B. Moods also result from various kinds of relationships with your important people.

As we have already remarked, changes in you during your teens produce changing relationships with others, such as parents, teachers, and other adults; with your peers, and especially with boys and girls. You have the adjustment to make of all these changes in your relationships.

You not only need to understand the changes that are taking place in you, but you also need to understand the effect of the changes on others, especially parents. As I have already noted, you have an ambivalence about growing up, that is, you both want to and do not want to. The same is true for your parents. Most of them are happy about the signs of increasing maturity and responsibility, but at the same time they cannot quite believe that it is happening and find it difficult to accept that you can do the things you can and should do. Their attitudes and expectations toward you usually lag behind your capacity and desire to move ahead. When your parents resist too strenuously your efforts to emancipate yourselves, if you are mentally and physically healthy, you will make still other and more vigorous attempts to break free and become your own person. These renewed efforts on your part to break the old ties and patterns may cause you to behave even more defiantly, thus further alarming and stiffening your parents' resistance to what you are trying to accomplish. Finally, both you and your parents lose the whole point of the struggle, with the result that both of you are frustrated and resentful. We need to remember that it is not easy for either an individual or a nation to declare its independence, and sometimes a revolution has to be violent before independence is achieved.

As adolescents you also need to remember that others may not only have difficulty with *what* you are trying to do, but *how* you are trying to do it. It is hard for parents to accept your mistakes, and it is imperative that you have the freedom to make mistakes as a necessary part of learning. These struggles between you and your parents and other adults are a fertile source of all kinds of moods—moods of timidity, arrogance, confidence, discouragement, and achievement.

A part of your struggle at this time has to do with the development of your own sense of personal authenticity. Prior to this age you have been dependent upon the authority of others. Now you have come to the time in life when you are having to develop your own sense of authority. But the period of transition between obedience to outside authority and the exercise of your own is a troublesome one which produces moods of rebellion, resentment, and arrogance.

Still another part of the struggle at this time of life has to do with a specific fear that has not been mentioned earlier: the fear of others and the fear for oneself. You are still dependent upon others for help, acceptance, and guidance. You now realize that people are not altogether trustworthy, that their thought and action can be injurious to you, and you have developed a fear of others. The fear of others inevitably means that you fear for yourselves; that, because of other people's failures to love and care, you will be hurt; that you will have to live defensively and will fail to become the kind of persons that you would like to be. These fears cause you to withdraw into isolation out of which come terrifying moods. These are usually moods of suspicion, resentment, and self-pity which produce in you behavior that only accentuates your problems, and thus there is born the well-known "vicious circle." The more fearful you become, the more defensive you act; the more defensive you are, the less free people are to love; the less free people are to love you, the more fearful you become for yourself. A practical question is: How do you break out of the vicious circle and overcome the moods that it produces? [1]

C. Your moods are also born out of the changes and pressures of the world in which you live.

Many moods are a result of conflict between your ac-

---

[1] See discussion on dialogue in chapter on resources for dealing with moods.

celerated physical and cultural growth and the continued refusal by society to grant to you many of the rights and opportunities of adults: When sexual desires are more powerful than they will ever again be, sexual opportunities are fewest; obedience and submission are asked of you at precisely the time when your strength, energy, and desire for autonomy are highest; responsible participation in the major social institutions is denied or discouraged at the moment when your interest in the world has been awakened. Your sense of injustice over society's withholding of opportunity must be tempered by the realization that there are good reasons for it. While you have powers for participation, these are not always balanced with the wisdom that more experience may bring. Nevertheless, the conflicts are a source of many of your moods.

The psychological and social pressures of the twentieth century also make short work of the innocence of childhood, and make adolescents aware early of the harsh realities of life. Your coming of age, more than at any other time, is in the midst of radical global transitions and transformations. Because of more widespread and constant communication from all sources, it is impossible for you not to be overly exposed to life as it is really lived. You are not permitted to remain naive as youth used to be. You have not been allowed the luxury of illusion or the satisfactions of disillusionment. The failures of approved institutions and the blunderings of the contemporary wise men are all too obvious to you. Your cynicism is understandable, and so is your bewilderment. Your potential for creativity is often hung in the balance. You are ready to express it, but how and where can you try it out. Who can guide you? You have to question the authorities that are commended to you, and yet you are not ready to exercise your own. The skills of others are inadequate, and your own skills are unformed and unfocused. And yet you face this confused world and its radical changes with courage, mixed, of course, with the inevitable confusions of the half-formed person. You peer anxiously into the past for possible clues to present behavior, as you also peer both arrogantly and anxiously into the future for signs of things to come and your part in them.

The energy of youth is obvious, and yet your perpetual motion is mixed with a lassitude and inertia because of the ambivalence you see all about you and which you experience within yourself. You are the product of revolutions in every area of life. Science has changed your view of the world and of yourselves and has increased your technological knowledge and skill with which even greater changes will be produced. Urban development which results from technological revolution is changing your values and way of life. The relative simplicity of familial relationships is giving way to the anonymous complexity of urban technical industrial existence. Many of you are being lost in this modern shuffle and you all fear getting lost yourselves. From these conditions stem all kinds of moods.

Present-day youth is confronted by another question. How can you choose your place and purpose in life when the work situation of man is changing so radically? You are told that in a few years there will be no connection between a man's work and his income because of changes resulting from the cybernetic revolution. You naturally wonder about a world in which men will receive the means for living independently of any job they may hold. If this is true, new incentives have to be found, new concepts formulated. If the old competitive free enterprise system is to disappear, what kind of education do you need in order to qualify for the new world? And, are you receiving that kind of education now?

Again, the racial revolution that is freeing men from the effect of prejudice and privilege introduces strange possibilities in the social order. The effects of a hundred years of prejudice are being exposed and some men are beginning to realize that society cannot prosper when there are first- and second-class citizens. We have discovered, too, that prejudice is learned especially in youth. During the various racial crises in our own time we have observed that young people have held and played opposite attitudes and roles. Some have fanned the flames of prejudice; others have been active in the fight against it. The inevitable tension in race conflict may breed in you moods of prejudice, hatred, and discrimination.

Educational pressures affect the personal adequacy of modern youth. Some of you are willing and able to respond to the high academic demand, but many of you are not ready for the degree of competition and rate of learning required. Many of you acquire a disabling sense of inadequacy because of competition for the highest grades, or because you are rejected by elite schools and colleges. The pressure for "academic excellence" often has inhumanizing effects on you as persons, and produces negative moods. Jerry's protest sounds loud and clear at this point: "Things are getting tougher . . . and everybody's always yelling about grades . . . And there's a heck of a lot more to learn, too."

Again, moods are created by the conflict that young people experience in a world in which things are often thought to be more important than persons. Your experiences of love suggest that persons are to be loved and things are to be used. Instead, you find that you are living in a culture in which things are more apt to be loved and persons used. More money, for example, is available for the exploration of space than for the exploration of human relations and the education of persons. You also resent being used instead of being loved, and you may sense that you are being trained in the practice of using people instead of loving them, from which comes your gradually acquired incapacity to love. At the same time you find it hard to accept that you have a functional role in life. You should expect to be used in the sense that a part of your purpose in life is to be useful to others. But there is an inevitable tension between being loved and being used. You can learn to respond to that tension in two constructive ways: Try to remember that the one whose function you use is also a person to be respected; and you can offer your own function to others as an expression of your own person. Thus, while you carry out the business of living in responsible functional relationship, you will also experience from time to time a real sense of personal relationship. The conflict one experiences between being used and being loved is another source of moods. Being used produces moods of unhappiness and resentment; experiences of love and real meeting between persons create moods of happiness and fulfillment.

D. Finally, you experience pressures to conform that stifle your originative and creative powers and thus produce disabling moods. Although the present age is a time of great freedoms, you still face the question: How much should you conform to the expectations and demands of the adult world and of your peers? Coupled with this is youth's inevitable fight against tradition in the matter of beliefs and morals and practices. Mary's experience with her mother about being a lady witnesses to this kind of pressure. Mary wanted to be her own kind of lady and not her mother's. But modern youth experiences also peer pressures to conform. "Don't be a square," is a standard for behavior. Drinking is so common that it seems impossible for many young people to refuse a drink without looking like a "party pooper." Driving is no longer just for transportation but a way of showing how bold one can be in defying the laws of nature and man, preferably with plenty of pals and gals who will do anything rather than risk being called "chicken." In the area of sex both boys and girls are hard put to resist the pressure to conform. Boys are expected to "make out" or "go all the way" with their dates, and girls feel that they have to meet their boyfriends' expectations if they are to be popular. Furthermore, "everybody's doing it."

Thus the demand from the older generation to conform to the standards and expectations of yesterday and the demands of present-day behavior exerted by peers produce in many of you tensions and conflicts which are the source of many different kinds of moods and also desperate behaviors.

You may notice an opposite response illustrated by Bill's. He remembers his moods of fear and inadequacy. In addition to the difficulties he had in relation to the adult world he acknowledges the help he has had from them. "I had a lot of help from Dad . . . his confidence in me never wavered . . . from Mother, too, before she died . . . and old Mr. Jim, the math teacher, who taught me to think . . . and Purdy, the coach. . . . These people all stood for something . . . just the thought of them gives me something to think about and live for."

Bill's reference to his indebtedness to people who "stood for something" points to another source of moods. There *is* something within and beyond our relationships to each other that influences us. The name God symbolizes what we are trying to identify: His Presence is in the midst of our life. We experience His Presence by a deep longing to be at one with Him and others. Our sense of incompleteness cries out for completion. We sense that there are values beyond those we understand and can measure. Our guilt asks for a love to restore beyond the power of human love. You may first experience such a sense of God during your teen years. This sense can produce in you moods of peace and serenity or moods of disturbance and anxiety. As a result of them you can experience either a greater closeness to life or an opposite one of impatience and separation. The sense of closeness in response to a sense of God is not hard to understand, but why should it also cause you feelings of separation and pain? The reason is not hard to find. The experience of God's presence is a challenging and disturbing one, just as a meeting with a truly great person may cause you to pull back out of fear and a sense of unworthiness. Such a response may be accompanied by feelings that are unpleasant both for you and others. In the midst of these experiences you may develop a deep sense of wrong and guilt which produce in you depressive and despondent moods accompanied by cynicism toward yourself, others, and life in general. On the other hand, a sense of guilt, when acknowledged, may produce a sense of peace and freedom for stronger and more courageous action.

Thus, your moods are caused by forces operating within you in response to changed conditions and relationships in a changing world.

We turn next to a consideration of your purposes and their effect on your moods.

power of purposes over moods

"I wish Dad would let me drive the car or I could afford one of my own . . . shucks, some guys can. . . . I hate being picked up by Mom. It's hard to act like a man when you're being carted around by a woman . . . she's always fussing over me as if I was a little kid.

Women are funny. I don't understand them. You never know what they're going to do. Take Janie . . . she likes to hold hands sometimes . . . other times she gets mad at me and really clams up. A couple of times I've held her real tight . . . pressed real close I could feel her against me . . . and we'd kiss. . . . I'd run my hands up and down her back, and once I felt the sides of her breasts, and then she'd break away and say that we shouldn't. Gee, it sure did feel good and I'm sure she liked it too. I'm glad she stopped, though . . . I mean, I was getting scared and wasn't sure what to do next. Well, this is part of what's getting me down. Why am I so damned dumb? I hear the other guys . . . they're always talking about "making out" with their dates . . . they seem to know their way around. Wonder if some of it is big talk? I know I talk big sometimes, and I'm always afraid some of the gang will find out I can't back it up."—*Jerry*

"Ma's too busy, and she never listens. . . . Dad's always working in his shop or at some meeting. Both of them are always pushing me . . . they say I'll never amount to anything unless I get going. But I don't want to go anywhere . . . I just want to stay here . . . but I wish it were different."—*Jake*

"I wish I knew who I am. I sometimes look in the mirror and wonder, what is me? I'm not always the same . . . with adults I'm different than I am with my own crowd . . . and then I'm still something else inside me (privately) . . . are these all the same me? There are times when I'm afraid that no one of these selves is really me . . . then I'm afraid I'll never find out who I am.

Another thing, I hate myself when I try to be the kind of person somebody else wants me to be. Being me is awfully complicated. And it's getting more complicated. I feel so different than I used to. I notice it most when I'm with Bill. He thinks I'm special, too. Wonder if he really loves me . . . he says he does. Anyhow, he makes being me being a girl. Always before I was just a person, and now I'm a *girl* person. Being a girl has become something special . . . but it's both wonderful and scary. I guess I'm becoming a woman."—*Mary*

"Dad wanted me to go to his school. He was a big name there but I want to make my own way.

Lately I've begun to think that I can be a part of something tremendous and much bigger than any of us. I want to be a part of it. . . . It's like being a part of a team . . . behind the scenes but very much a part of it. Someone like the coach . . . like in a game . . . I want to throw myself into it not caring what happens as long as we play well, and yet wanting to win. . . . But what is winning in this new game that I seem to be joining?"—*Bill*

A moody person is one who is the victim of his moods without any power over them. Like a rudderless ship he moves at the whim and mercy of every wind and current that blows and flows. A moody person, therefore, is one who has nothing to steer him. One of your best resources for steering comes from having purposes for living. You can be largely motivated by them, and your intentions in relation to them can keep you organized and moving. If you have purposes such as studying for a chosen work or becoming a certain kind of person you will be better able to throw off negative moods and to cultivate positive ones. What are some of these purposes?

One very primary purpose is to acquire a sense of yourself as an achieving person. Such a sense comes from experiences of accomplishment. Early in the last chapter we identified three fundamental tasks that need to be accomplished. First, the task of freeing yourselves from the old filial dependencies and the achievement of powers of self-reliance and self-direction. This was what Jerry was wrestling with when he complained about being picked up by his mother. "It's hard to act like a man when you're being carted around by a woman . . . she's always fussing over me as if I were a kid." A second task is to complete your sexual development and become heterosexual adults whose primary interest and capacity is in relation to the opposite sex. Jerry and Mary are obviously working out this problem. Jerry and Janie are feeling their way into a more mature expression of the relation between men and women. And Mary is wrestling with the meanings of being a woman which come into focus because of Bill. And the third task is to decide what in the world you are to do, and where in the world you will do it. The accomplishment of these three tasks is the work of youth, and as you work at them you will become an emerging adult. It takes courage for you to emerge as an adult and a responsible human being who is able to submerge your own needs and interests, without ignoring them altogether, in the service of the needs of others.

You will not accomplish the foregoing tasks in a year or two because, if you remain a growing person, you will work at them all your life. You can make such progress in the accomplishment of these tasks, however, that early in your life you can begin to experience yourself as an achieving person. It is quite possible for you to learn to love achieving more than the contemplation of achievements. Of course, it is always wonderful to be able to look back with satisfaction on a work that you have at least partially completed. When you can recognize and accept what you have done you gain confidence in yourself which further nurtures strength and courage for keeping at the job.

It is also exciting to have things to do, and to enjoy working at them with the expectation that with the help of others you will achieve. Important as the accomplishment of a task is, the acquisition of confidence in yourself as an achiever is of even greater importance.

Being an achiever does not mean that you never fail. Jerry's youthful fear of failure, as he undertakes a new responsibility or skill, can be reassured by the experiences of countless men. Winston Churchill's life, for example, was strewn with failures in the midst of his achievements, but he was not afraid to take the risks that also led to his successes. In order to achieve you will have to take chances. Learning to drive a car is an illustration. Of course, it is good to know how to drive with skill and safety. It is an even greater achievement, though, to have overcome your fears, to have learned the necessary disciplines, and to have achieved the ability and right to operate an automobile, especially when you do it without accident and harm to yourself and others. Such achievements contribute to the accomplishment of still another purpose.

A second purpose is to acquire a dependable sense of your own identity. It is important that you should know who you are, and to learn that you and others can count on your being the same person under all kinds of conditions. One of the great modern students of identity, Dr. Erik Erikson,[1] says that identity is a sense of sameness, a

---

[1] Erikson, Erik H, "The Problem of Ego Identity," in Stein. Maurice, *et al.,* eds., *Identity and Anxiety* (New York: The Free Press of Glencoe, Inc., 1960).

unity and dependability of personality that is formed in the individual and recognized by others.

We grow our sense of identity through all the years of our lives. In the beginning when we are children our sense of identity is not distinguishable to any great extent from that of our parents, although it is obvious even in these earlier years that we wrestle with the problem of being ourselves apart from the being of others. You gather meaning for your use of "I" until "I" stands for you with a singularity and distinctness but in the context of your relation and commonness with others who also have some degree of identity.

Mary is struggling to establish her own sense of identity. "I wish I knew who I am . . . I'm afraid I'll never find out." In the last chapter we noted her attempt to be herself as distinct from her mother. "This is why I fight with Mom . . . she wants me to be a lady . . . I can't be her kind of lady. I'd rather be me." Now, she adds, "Being me is awfully complicated. . . . [Because of Bill,] being a girl has become something special . . . but it's both wonderful and scary. I guess I'm becoming a woman."

The formation of a sense of identity is often greatly accelerated when you are forced to pass through some kind of crisis such as starting school, moving into high school or college, your first date, being jilted, disobedience and punishment at home, your first difficulties with the police, failure or unbelievable success, the death of someone you love, and so on. Your crisis both tests whatever identity you have been able to achieve and gives you opportunity to use your resources. The experience may then make further contributions to your understanding of who you are and what your powers are.

Your achievement of identity is of profound importance

and is crucial for your development. Youngsters, for example, who have not found themselves and have a weak sense of who they are, are often rebellious, uneasy, and susceptible to all kinds of crazy suggestions and schemes. The tragedy in these cases is not only in what they do but in the fact that their behavior means that they have not found themselves. Unfortunately, society often fails to give these individuals understanding and help because of reaction against their behavior, so that the situation of delinquent young persons is made worse by further identity confusions. Out of such confusions come all sorts of moods.

Baptism is concerned with identity. When you are baptized you are given a name to identify you as a person distinguishable from all others. In addition, your eternal relationships and inheritance are stated, that is, you are a "child of God, a member of Christ, and an inheritor of the Kingdom of God." How can you understand such a statement of identity? For many people baptism is only a form you go through because you belong to the church. Instead, it is supposed to initiate you into a group in which you are known as someone special, a group in which you are known as a unique person who has a special relation to God and all men. Baptism is also supposed to be a guarantee of your freedom to be a person in your own right, and to be known and supported by other people who are similarly recognized and bound together by the love and action of God. What these words mean will now be spelled out in human terms.

What are some characteristics of a sense of identity?

First, countenance. Countenance means face. Identity requires that you have a face of recognizable features. I do not mean "face" literally because, of course, you have a face. Instead, I mean that you are easily recognized as to who you are; that you are recognized always as the same person with constant and dependable characteristics. One of your responsibilities in all circumstances and conditions is to find your face, to acquire identifiable features which you know are your own by means of which others will recognize you.

Second, identity requires that you have a voice of your own, again, figuratively speaking. This means that you should be able to speak for yourself and will have the courage to do so. In contrast, many are afraid to speak up, or if they do speak, they speak in terms of pretenses and lies so that even they as well as others are never sure with what voice they are speaking. Or they may depend on others to speak for them—the "crowd," the union, the political party, the editorial comments of others. Your words are important because they represent you. Your words are the instrument of your relationships and they should honestly represent you. By your words you commit yourself to others. Your word is to be trusted, and it is out of such trust relationship your identity comes. And your task is to find your identity, to find your voice with which you can speak to others in relationships of trust. Bill has found his voice and, therefore, a part of his identity. Jake is afraid to speak up and is without identity except in terms of his resentment of those who he feels dominate him.

Third, identity means having your own place in the scheme of things. Bill had his place, but Jerry did not. He expressed his lack of a sense of "place" when he said that he wished he could have made the long run that Bill made in the game with Cedar High. "Then they would have cheered me instead of him. Me? What can I do?" As yet he does not feel that he has found himself anywhere. Such a place does not have to be big, but it has to be real. Not all men should or can have a prominent place. Wherever you are, make yourself at home there, make that place mean something because you are there, something that will make it a better place for others. Bill was clear that he did not want to go to his Dad's college. He said, "He (Dad) was a big name there but I want to make my own way." Some of Bill's friends warned him against any excessive show of enthusiasm by saying, "Down, Bill, down, or you'll get noticed and get in trouble." They were urging him to remain inconspicuous through conformity. Conformity means having no place of your own, and instead requires that everyone occupy the same place. The common place is no place at all. And your task now is to try and find your place in life and occupy it responsibly.

Fourth, identity means having a work with a purpose. By nature you need to be able to make something, do something, or serve someone. Unfortunately, many millions of people are only interested in earning some kind of living. They lack any overall purpose for their living. Failure here produces tremendous frustration with its inevitable accompaniment of negative moods. Your achievement of a sense of purpose is not a once and for all accomplishment. It is a growing and developing thing. It will take time to find, and will change during the course of your life. At one time your purpose may be to study and learn, or to get ahead and become established in a business or profession; to render service to people or causes; or to find a meaning for your life. Purpose can be found everywhere: not only by serving in the Peace Corps but by working as a salesman in Kresge's. Sometimes you may say of yourself, "I have no purpose," and yet you may be serving a purpose of which you are not yet conscious. Now, in your youth, your task is to find your place, your purpose, your mission, and to get educated and organized to serve them.

And, finally, I suggest that your sense of identity will

enable you to be with or against others. As we have indicated all along the line so far, relationship is terribly important, and your ability to stand judiciously with or against people, and to do so with respect for both them and yourself, is a great sign of identity.

A child of God, therefore, is one who is acquiring his face, voice, place, work, and capacity to live with people. These are among the ways in which you will have identity not only as a person but as a member of Christ.

Your identity is always being challenged by the changes that go on in the outside world. You experienced these changes when, as children, you were moved from one community or school to another. Wars and political and social upheavals also produce changes that test your identity and cause anxiety and either defensive apathy or active aggression. We see apathy in Jake's response to his life, and constructive aggression in Bill's response to his.

There are three reactions to change that are destructive to identity. First, you may try to intellectualize the difficulty away, and talk yourself out of dilemmas. You will face temptations to be glib. You may want to substitute thinking for doing, and may make the mistake of thinking that when you have talked about something you have done it.

Another response to the threat of change and upheaval is that of wandering, that is, you seek to escape by moving from place to place, from job to job, from friend to friend. You keep on the go and are afraid to stop. You may be always looking for some other place or some other thing to do in order to evade dealing with the threat or change.

Another destructive response to the dangers of change is the merchandising one. You are tempted to evaluate people and things in terms of what they are worth, and what they can do, especially for you. This marketing way of life can become a substitute for personal human relations. You may seek to turn persons into things, and to value things above persons. God's purpose is that persons are to be loved and things are to be used, but we often change the relationship to one in which we love things and use people.

There are some dangers to be avoided in the process of achieving your identity. Try to avoid confusion of identity which can cause you to get hung up on issues and not be able to make your decisions about them. In a desperate effort to pull out of a stall you may make impulsive decisions with unfortunate results that cannot be reversed. This is Jake's plight. His lack of sense of identity keeps him from being able to decide even to shovel the walk.

Then there is what Dr. Erikson calls identity diffusion, which is really the spreading of yourselves so thin that you do not have to come to grips with anything. So much of you is spread over so many activities and responsibilities that you cannot pull yourself together for decisive action.

There is another danger which Dr. Erikson calls identity foreclosure. When you foreclose on identity you are expressing a fear of finding out who you are. You do this, for example, by playing it safe, by eliminating from your life possibilities of change or any new and different experiences. If you foreclose on or avoid opportunities, you will develop rigid and opinionated attitudes, and view the meaning of life from within the limits of ever deepening ruts.

The development of a sense of identity depends upon your growing ability to make personal, occupational, sexual, and idea commitments. These have to be made, of course, out of a wide variety of possibilities. Your choices benefit you when you make your choices out of a variety of possibilities and gradually single out a few things to which you fully give yourself. Some people choose prematurely and become bored; others never really choose and do not really give themselves to anyone or anything with the result that they only fritter away their life.

The answer to the question, what kind of person are you, is important. The kind of person you are determines your behavior, although other people and circumstances also influence your behavior. Even so, your behavior will reflect your character which will show even when you are under pressure. Your doing will be an expression of what you are. If your identity is that of an achiever, that is, one who gets things done, you will not have the same struggles with the temptations to waste time as a nonachiever does. Such a way of life prevents the occurrence of many negative moods and opens you to the possibility of positive ones. A sense of identity helps you to be both flexible and stable. This thought leads to a third purpose of youth's work.

A third purpose is your achievement of a sense of integrity. If you are a person with integrity, you are one who is both whole and honest, that is, you hang together as one, and you are what you seem to be. Because of your integrity you will have some power over your moods. The opposite of a person with integrity is one who tries to be different things to different people, and also pretends to be what he is not. Such a person is spineless, weak, and undependable. He lacks virtue. Many of you shy away from the concept of virtue because you associate it with prissiness.

Virtue means strength, manliness, and stands in sharp contrast to all moralistic "goody-goody" concepts. Virtue that is vital rather than moralistic is great! Virtue that is vital means a quality that is always related to the deepest and best meanings of life. Sometimes morality and life seem to fight each other. We often feel the tension between the demands of life and those of a moral code. Jesus himself often stood on the side of life and against the moralists. He stood on the side of the woman who was taken in adultery by reproving the moralists and saying to them, "Let him that is without sin cast the first stone." But neither did he approve adultery because he said to the woman, "Go, sin no more."

Jerry experienced these tensions in his relations with Janie. On the one hand he was responding to his newly acquired need for intimacy with members of the opposite sex and felt a natural urge to explore these new powers and feelings. On the other hand, the question of morality was experienced through Janie's inhibitions that represented both the adult world's teaching about the relation between boys and girls, and her own sense of integrity in relation to herself and him. You remember he experienced a certain relief when the expression of her inhibitions brought their explorations to a stop for the time being. They are two young people who, with a sense of identity that is still being formed, are responding to and forming a sense of integrity.

Here again we see the need of a tension between variety and faithfulness. A variety of experiences is necessary for the development of the individual, and yet, within those many possibilities, decisions have to be made in terms of faithfulness both to oneself and to others. You cannot go it alone. You cannot accomplish your purposes by exploiting others, and you begin to see here that the achievement of both identity and integrity grow out of relationships with each other that are both free and structured.

In the achievement of both a sense of identity and integrity you are dependent upon people who stand for something beside their own immediate satisfaction and desire for success. You see the effect of this on Jerry and Mary and Bill. Their parents are people who have convictions, who meet life responsibly, who can accept both success and failure, who do not crumble if they do not get their own way, and who love their children enough to let them be responsible for themselves. The young person of either sex who has worthy adults to emulate and who feels admired by those who trust him has an inner sense of stability and can weather all kinds of crises. Remember that Bill spoke of his appreciation of his father and mother, and of his coach, and of his science teacher. They seem to have had a tremendous influence on his life.

And there is evidence that because he had this kind of example, Bill himself is becoming the kind of person who stands for something. His identity is now beginning to be contributed to by values that come to him from outside himself. He thinks in terms of his purposes, of the possibilities of life, in terms of frontiers where he might live and work. Jerry will probably move in that direction, too. And it is also clear that the character of Mary's struggles in becoming a woman and her thoughts about marriage or a career indicate that she is forming a focus that will give her power for the decisions she will have to make all her life.

Such relationships are the kind that baptism intends when it refers to our membership in Christ and our being inheritors of the Kingdom: relationships of love, understanding, support, guidance, forgiveness, and trust. Through such relationships we experience the presence and love and action of God.

Knowing who you are, and being true to who you are as you mature and grow in the midst of the changes and challenges of your life, determines and controls your moods, and provides a basis for growth and development of creative powers.

A fourth purpose that you may serve and that will help you control your moods is to join the world and be a participant-contributor to its life and work. Youth's struggle between rebellion against the past and his resignation in response to the difficulties of the present shows his concern for selfhood and integrity. You need to do your own thinking. You are working out your identity and creating your own standards. You are a participant in your own revolution against the things as they are. There are risks in such activity, including the possibility that you may lose yourself. But if you will not take these risks, you cannot emerge as a creative adult. A creative adult is one who is able finally to take his place in the world with creative potential and participate in the shaping of the history of his own time. To be a shaper of history is to be an inheritor and participant in the Kingdom of God. A Christian is supposed to be a participant in the Kingdom and a shaper of history. Whether or not you realize your creative potential as man made by God depends in part on how you are met. You are not only born into a family but into a church, and into the stream of life in the making. You may think that what you do from day to day does not matter, but it does. In this flow of event and meaning that has been going on for centuries and will continue long after you have departed, you are a new event having within yourself creative powers. Education, formal and informal, is the process in which you are met and helped to become yourself in responsible relation to persons, the things and processes of life, and God who is both apart from all that he made and acts through it all.

Your drive to achievement, your sense of identity and

integrity, will pull into creative coordination the power of your moods. Youngsters with purposes do not have the same conflicts and struggles as do those without them because they know who they are, who they serve, what they want to do, and they are able to engage in behavior appropriate to their identity and purposes. If negative moods overtake them, they have the resources with which to re-direct them and certainly to survive them. These same re-sources will help to produce in you, in the midst of the crises and changes of your lives, positive moods. Their energy and meaning will, in turn, add to your resourcefulness.

resources for dealing with moods

"Me? What can I do? Dad says, though, that my day will come."—*Jerry*

Somebody's always breathing down my neck. I wish I belonged to another family like Jerry's . . . you can tell Jerry's Dad likes him. And his mother's great . . . she doesn't nag him all the time."—*Jake*

"You can count on Dad . . . he practices what he preaches . . . Gad, he sure did believe in me.
When I get angry with my girl friend and tell her what's on my mind, even if I hurt her, we then often understand each other better. Then she does the same thing, and that helps us too."—*Bill*

We come now to the most important parts of this book, the parts having to do with the resources for dealing with your moods, and with suggestions as to how to use them. It is hard for us to know what our resources are because our problems are easier to see. Jerry, for example, said, "Me? What can I do? Dad says, though, that my day will come."

It is not necessary for you always to suffer your moods. You can undergo changes that in turn change your moods and give you power over them. You can use in more con-

73

structive ways than in moodiness the energy and meaning contained in your moods. I have some suggestions that may help you in these accomplishments. My suggestions will be offered under three headings: Accept your moods; dialogue with life instead of fighting and fleeing from it; and become a part of something that is much bigger than yourself or your moods.

First, learn to accept your moods. Moods, as we have seen, are an inevitable part of your life. They cannot be avoided, nor should they be even if avoidance were possible. Moods give variety to your emotional existence and reassure you that you are alive and responding to your various environments.

Acceptance of your moods gives you power over them. Acceptance does not mean that you approve of them, but it does mean that your moods are an expected part of your life, that they belong to you, that you have a responsibility to be as creatively responsive to them as you can be. Sometimes people try to ignore their moods or pretend that they do not exist. This leaves the mood free to operate, which it often does to the detriment of the person's well being.

Moods are also useful. They are signs to be read, signs that tell you and others about yourself and how you are doing. They express nonverbally what you cannot say verbally. Nevertheless, not all of the meaning of your moods is available to you or evident to others. One of the hard things about life is that our inner meanings and needs remain unrecognized and unmet. And one of the purposes of human relationships is to be alert and responsive to the meanings and needs of others. Within limits, however, it is possible for us to interpret the meaning of moods. An irritable mood tells you that you have been frustrated by something or someone. Jake was in this kind of mood when, referring to his parents, he said, "Both of them are always pushing me . . . they say I'll never amount to anything unless I get going. But I don't want to go anywhere . . . I just want to stay here . . . but I wish things were different." He also expressed the mood of anger and panic in response to his parents' suggestion that he go to church because it would be good for him and make him behave. You remember he said, "I hit the roof. I'm sick of being told what I ought to do. Sometimes when I'm in church I can hardly breathe. . . . I want to rush out of there to where I can breathe again, and fling my arms, and run and shout, and be free. Now they've taken away a part of my allowance. God, I hate them! . . . I wish they'd drop dead."

Then there are the moods of excitement and elation indicating that you are in good relation with your important people, parents, teachers, peers, and others. We saw this in Bill who said, "I've begun to think that I can be a part of something tremendous. . . . I sense an excitement growing within me that makes it impossible for me to 'play it cool.' "

There are also the moods of inadequacy expressed several times by Jerry and Mary which tell us of the difficulties they had in measuring up to their own and others' concept of them, and of the trouble they had keeping up with their peers.

Some people only suffer from their moods. Others learn to understand moods and because of the understanding do something constructive about the causes of them. Jerry was encouraged by his father's saying, "Your day will come." In the meantime, he is working at living as a sixteen-year-old should, that is, he has developed a sense of purpose and a growing determination which enables him to follow the examples of his parents and others. At the same time he has mixed feelings about school and its requirements, about adults and the way they live. These experiences cause him to wonder whether he will ever make the grade, and produce in him feelings of discouragement and lassitude. But the negative side of his feelings is often carried by the positive side. Here we have an insight that is important for us all: everything has both a negative and a positive side. Hostility is the negative side of love. Love is the important thing and is the source of life. You can resent those you love and who love you, and the expression of your resentment toward them is a negative expression of the love that you would give and receive. Try to realize that the expression of hostility is not a denial of love but is a dark and strange expression of it.

This relation of opposites to each other is spoken of in a book that is popular among many young people—*The Prophet* by Kahlil Gibran.[1] When asked about the relation of joy and sorrow, Gibran replied,

"Joy is your sorrow unmasked.

And the self same well from which your laughter rises was oftentimes filled with your tears.

The deeper the sorrow carves into your being, the more joy you can contain.

Is not the cup that holds your wine the very cup that was burned in the potter's oven.

When you are joyous, look deep in your heart and you shall find it is only that which has given you sorrow that is giving you joy.

When you are sorrowful, look again in your heart and you shall see that in truth you are weeping for that which has been your delight.

Some of you say joy is greater than sorrow, others say, Nay, sorrow is the greater.

But I say unto you, they are inseparable."

[1] Published by Alfred A. Knopf (New York, 1923). Used by permission.

And so is the relation between love and hate. Of love, the same prophet says,

"He who loves must expect to bleed willingly and joyfully.
For even as love crowned you so shall he crucify you."

Only as we learn this lesson can we hope to read the signs of our moods. Looked at on the surface, depression seems to add up only to negative suffering. But behind the surface darkness of depression there are other meanings that reach toward light. Depressions represent the momentary response of someone who is wrestling with life vs. death, truth vs. lies, and hope vs. despair.

A fever is as much a symptom of health as of illness because it is caused by the body's healing powers fighting the forces of illness. So likewise our moods of disturbance are symptoms of your fight against thoughts and feelings and relationships that threaten you, and they represent your struggle toward life and purpose and hope.

This relation between dark and light, negative and positive, is caught up in the drama of the life of Christ. The crucifixion is the dark side and by itself is a symbol of suffering, failure and death, but the light side, represented by the Resurrection, is the symbol of life for us. This means that with the power of God we can bring life out of death, beauty out of ugliness, hope out of despair. All of this says that our greatest resource for destructive moods is in the indestructible, irrepressible power of life which men have identified as God.

Understanding of this death-life dialogue can lead you to an acceptance of negative moods as evidence of meaning and energy which is available to you for creative pursuit of your purposes. When you surrender to a mood you have given yourself completely to the negative side of things; but if you can remember that you are still related to positive possibilities you will be better able to stir yourself to greater hope, determination, and effort. Your mood of inadequacy is a necessary part of your struggle for adequacy. Thus, the meaning and energy of your mood can be redirected in a constructive way.

A second resource for dealing with your moods is dialogue. You may think of dialogue as parts said by various actors in a play. Dialogue is that, and more. It is also the honest talking out of an issue by two or more people who honestly hold their respective convictions, but who try to be open to the convictions of others. Dialogue is as necessary to relationship as air is to the body. Its power in relation to moods and other aspects of your life will be made clear in a moment. We need now to do a little reviewing.

You have seen through the pages that you have just read that your moods and other problems are often caused by your relationship with other people and by your response to them. A mood of inadequacy tells you that you have failed in some relationship, in the demands of that relationship, and in the skills needed to meet the demands. Parents and teachers sometimes expect and demand too much, and because you cannot measure up to their expectations you develop feelings of inadequacy. The mood may be made worse by your failure to evaluate their demand. An uncritical acceptance of an unreasonable demand may make you feel more inadequate than you are, that is, you may be more adequate than at the moment you seem to be. While you need to grow in your power to believe independently in yourself, you also need the understanding and support of others. Without this support your negative moods may cause you to resent others, to become alienated from them, and you find it impossible to deal honestly with the issues that troubled you in the first place.

One of the great things about Jesus was his acceptance and affirmation of people. He saw, as others did not, the good in men and their resourcefulness. His affirmation of them restored their self-respect and self-confidence. This same spirit of affirmation toward others is supposed to be characteristic of all Christians. Such relationships give life to others.

You cannot survive outside of relationship. When you are separated and alienated from people, you begin to die. You may not want to admit your dependence upon others; you may want to be able to "go it alone," and you may strive to be unreasonably independent. Yet you still have to depend upon others. Healing for your problems and moods are to be found in your relationships. We see this in Jake's longing for the kind of relationship that Jerry had with his father and mother. His anger against his own parents was an expression of the frustration of his own intense longing for their love and his buried love for them. We see it also in Bill's acknowledgement of what his parents and teachers and coach had meant to him as he worked through his various crises. Participation in relationship is the medicine for isolation that results from your fear of others and your fear for yourselves.

You cannot have healing and helpful relationships, however, without communication. Elsewhere, in another book,[2] I have written: "Dialogue is to love what blood is to the body. When the flow of blood stops, the body dies. When dialogue stops, love dies and resentment and hate are born. Dialogue can restore a dead relationship. Indeed, this is the miracle of dialogue. It can bring relationship into being and it can bring into being once again a relationship that has died."

The point of all this is that your moods are often a

[2] *The Miracle of Dialogue*, Seabury Press (New York, 1963).

symptom of disturbed relationships, and one way of dealing with such moods is through communication. In other words, you must be prepared to talk things through with the right people. Talking things through is what I mean by dialogue. In an earlier chapter [3] I raised the question: How do we break out of the vicious circles of human relationship? We cannot hope always to be successful in this matter, but any success we have in breaking out of vicious circles will result from an honest attempt at dialogue. A young man explained the point when he said, "When I get angry with my girl friend and tell her what's on my mind, even if I hurt her, we then often understand each other better. Sometimes she does the same thing, and that helps us, too."

These human illustrations of the importance of dialogue help us understand the purpose of Christ in history. Men's relations to God and man had become religiously stiff and formal, grim, and hard. Christ lived among men simply and freely. He listened to them while he lived their life and spoke to them about the meaning of life in their own rather than in religious terms. His simple honest love frightened them and they killed him. He accepted death at their hands as a part of the dialogue; but what he was could not be killed, and our doctrine of the Resurrection is a way of saying that though men thought they killed him, he still lives. The dialogue that he is and employed brings and renews life. Our faith in him and the practice of it in our relations with each other is a resource for dealing with our problems, including our moods. Our faith in him is best expressed by keeping our relations with each other open, and we can do this by staying in communication with each other.

[3] See What causes moods? p. 43.

As you talk things through you try to do a number of things. You try to say what you think and feel with as much honesty as you can and with as much consideration of others as you can muster, that is, "speak the truth in love." You say what you have to say as clearly as possible and refrain from saying any more than is necessary. And you try to refrain from saying things that unnecessarily hurt other people.

In dialogue you also try to leave the other person free to speak for himself. One of the blocks to communication is our tendency to carry on both sides of a conversation, and seek to influence people's responses in ways that are favorable to our own interests. In so using people we arouse their resentment, and cloud the issues of our relationship so that they are never dealt with. Instead, we need to learn to speak *and* listen *and* heed what we hear.

A final step in dialogue is to be prepared to deal with other people's responses, whatever they are, with the hope that through give-and-take the issue will be cared for. We might summarize the process by saying that you have to speak honestly, listen carefully, hear accurately, and respond courageously to what you have heard. This kind of process makes both you and the person to whom you are talking free, and clears up rather than further confuses your questions and issues.

You have a number of resources for this kind of communication. First, you have eyes and ears. It may seem too obvious to say that eyes are to be used for seeing and ears for hearing, but it is true that too many people have eyes that see not and ears that hear not. The other resource you have for communication is your mouth which is for speaking responsibly. Speaking responsibly calls for a coordinated use of eyes, ears, and mouth. Much of our talking confuses matters because we speak only with our mouths and without assistance of eyes and ears. Your eyes and ears give you clues as to what you might say. Someone has observed that we were given two eyes and two ears and one mouth to indicate that eyes and ears ought to be used more than the mouth. Translated, this means that seeing and hearing must precede speaking.

Dialogue may be used as a way of working out understandings and relationships with your peers and adults. When you get in a bind with someone try to pay attention to him and his concerns as well as to yourself and your concerns. Ask yourself, "What is eating him? Why does he feel the way he does? What is he trying to say about himself and his situation? What values is he trying to offer me?" It is only by talking things through, sharing understandings, and persistent exchange that the differences between you and others can be resolved or adjusted, fears allayed, defenses broached, and trust built. Two-way communication teaches you to accept help and to give it, to trust and to be trustworthy, and to be both independent and reasonably dependent. Out of your dialogue will come clarifications, insights, new perspectives, and personal help. The more capacity you have for dialogical communication, the more power you will have over your negative moods because they are often an expression of your sense of isolation. Dialogue also develops in you the positive and affirmative moods that spring out of fruitful relationships.

In the course of consulting with young people while I was writing this book, I asked them what they did when they were caught in disturbing moods. Many of them replied that they found conversations with others most helpful, even though at the time they might have real resistance to being verbally responsive. They had, however, a sense of someone reaching out to draw them up out of the emotional hole into which they had fallen. In the case of anger moods, they acknowledged that expression of anger followed by discussion of its effects often brought about reconciliation. Moods of inadequacy likewise were helped by dialogue with people who were willing and able to discuss the problem with them.

a resource you are afraid to use

"When Dad and Ma said that I ought to go to church, that it would make me act more like other people, I hit the roof. I'm sick of being told what I ought to do. Sometimes when I'm in church I can hardly breathe. . . . I want to rush out of there to where I can breathe again, and fling my arms, and run and shout, and be free."—*Jake*

"Lately I've begun to think that I can be a part of something tremendous and bigger than any of us. I want to be a part of it. . . . I want to throw myself into it not caring what happens as long as we play well, and yet wanting to win. . . . But what is winning in this new game that I seem to be joining. Our minister thinks I'm discovering the religious dimension of my life. Maybe . . . I can't follow the church's ideas, but if there's something there I'd like to find it. It's as if some part of me is going to join up with another part of me. I sense an excitement growing within me that makes it impossible to 'play it cool.' I don't want to keep things 'cool.'—*Bill*

Continuing the discussion of resources we turn to a third resource for your moods, namely, religious *faith*. Before you turn away, I ask you to think with me about this matter first and then make up your minds.

Many of you admit that you have a lot of resistance to religion, and at the same time that you have strong religious feelings. Apparently you are suspicious that older people will try to make you accept their forms of belief.

Many of you find formal religion does not make sense to you. It seems that the religion you rebel against is a religion of rules and regulations that wants to make you conform to things as they are.

You may remember that Jake reacted against this conformist, moralistic kind of religion. He rebelled when his father and mother told him that he ought to go to church, that it would be good for him, and make him behave. You remember his comment, "Sometimes when I'm in church I can hardly breathe . . . I mean, I want to rush out of there to where I can breathe again, and fling my arms, and run and shout, and be free." Many people find religion to be like a small closet into which the meanings of life are stuffed. One of the reasons why God doesn't figure more in their lives is that their concept of him is too small. This kind of religion produces depressed and disturbing moods that incapacitate people for life and love.

True religion is something else. It means not less but more life, not less but more freedom, not less but more love. True religion loves life and helps people to live it freely and daringly. Jesus taught and practiced that kind of religion. In his day, as in ours, certain kinds of religious people lived by rules and regulations. For example, they taught that you should not work on the Sabbath; and that if you did, you would provoke God's displeasure. They accused him of breaking the religious law about the Sabbath because he healed a woman on that day. They did not like his ignoring of religious rules and customs in the interest of his love and care of persons. They resented his acceptance of sinners because sinners had broken moral and religious laws. They were out to get him because he would not conform to their laws and conventions. Furthermore, he claimed that his love and care for all kinds of people represented God more than did their religious rules and ceremonies. We have the same tensions today.

There are church people whose practice of religion is more concerned with the little matters of religious observance than with the love of people and the deeper meanings of their lives. There are some, for example, who do not want young people to use the church building for gatherings because their activities might injure the property. Again, young people are sometimes not allowed to dance on church property because they might do "things that are wrong." These are examples of the kinds of legalisms and moralisms that are contrary to a Christian spirit.

Fortunately, not all church people are of that kind. Instead, they are kind, considerate, accepting, and bring into human relations qualities that make life good for themselves and others.

You also have questions about belief, especially belief in God. Your problem seems to be that you don't want beliefs to be imposed on you. As one of you said, "The formal concepts of God mean so little to kids." It also seems true that you cannot believe without having a lot of doubts but that you think adults, especially ministers and teachers, do not have them. Doubt always accompanies growth and is essential to the development of faith. We Christians believe that Jesus Christ revealed what God is like but there were times when he doubted, too. One of the best prayers you can pray is, "Lord, I believe; help thou my unbelief." If you can learn to accept doubt as a part of believing, you will be better able to prevent the moods caused by doubt that are unassisted by belief. A good example of what we are talking about is to be found in a teen-ager who believes that his parents love him. Nevertheless, he sometimes questions whether they really do. His doubt is a part of his faith in them; and his doubt is carried by his faith in them. He also knows that he has to believe in them, just as in all of us there is a need to believe in something or someone, unless our capacity to believe has been destroyed. So believe by also searching and questioning. It is my conviction that Jesus would find your questioning search for truth more congenial than some religious people's rigid and closed adherence to their beliefs.

Sometimes we forget that the word "God" and our words about God are not God as he is. Those words are only symbols that point to a being and a meaning that we can never fully know or understand. God in himself is not a being who can be figured out. God is to be trusted, not proven; just as anyone you love is to be trusted and not proven. The various arguments for the existence of God are interesting and may be of some intellectual help, but your sense of God is more apt to be born out of the meanings that you forge out of your living. As one teenager put it, "If God is, he must have something to do with love." While this insight may sound trite, you need to remember that all kinds of people working in the various fields of study, especially those studying human need and meaning all come up with love as being the most important thing in life. All this study and experience seems to say that the Being behind everything is love. All our creativeness, our need and our understanding seem to point to this truth. And this is what the Bible says, "God is love." Here is the best medicine for bad moods!

Another block to your acceptance of religion seems to be that it presents itself in ways that make you fearful. So much of religion seems to be concerned with death which to you is intolerable, with judgment and authority which you resent, with suffering and pain which naturally you want to shun. You dislike, therefore, many religious symbols especially when they are presented as having literal meaning, such as hell, cross of Christ, blood, law of God. All these things and their symbols are truly terrifying if we do not see them in the context of God's love. Your own experience of human love tells you that the judgment of someone who loves you is supportive as well as painful. The cross of Christ is not just a symbol of suffering and death but a new life and victory that comes when we give ourselves to others and to causes. Instead of making us afraid and resentful, religious faith can reassure and strengthen us for more courageous living, and thus dispel destructive moods.

All Christians, young or old, are called to be daring, courageous, and compassionate. A Christian is meant to live by the spirit of Jesus rather than by the rules of religion. He lives by trying to participate in the kind of activities he associates with God: creation, healing, and making all things new.

How do we participate in the creation, healing, and renewing activity of God? If we believe that God is the being behind all being, behind all manifestations of life, and that His creation action is a continuing action, we can also believe that our living in the world can be participation in His purposes and work. Your study in school —mathematics, for example—can be understood as a searching out of the nature of things in order that you may appreciate, another word for worship, and employ, another word for serve, what has been created. You have a responsibility to explore, know, and use mathematics. Again, all the thousands of people who are contributing to the exploration of space are engaged in a profound sense in a religious activity. In order to send men into space it is necessary for other men to study the nature of many things, to unravel the created universe, and to learn how to use its energy and other resources. Because of our careful, another word for reverent, study of the universe and its forces, and because of our growing ability to use them, we are better able to understand the nature of God and to honor Him than men have ever been before. This is true because we have traced out more of the mysteries of His creation. How much more wonderful God seems now in the light of our present understanding of Him and His creation than He seemed when it was thought that He had created only the sun and the moon and the earth, and had done so in six days! All scientific achievements, there-fore, can be understood to have religious significance, and those who participate in them can be understood as participating in the creative activity of God.

People who build and who adorn, who maintain and repair, who work in form and color and sound to increase the joy and meaning of life are also participants in the creation of God. In choosing your work you may choose it in response to this kind of religious understanding, and in so doing provide channels for the creative expression of your moods.

We also believe that God is concerned for the relations between man and man which have implicit in them man's relation to Him. He is concerned with the healing of hos-tility, with the breaking down of barriers that separate men, and with the restoration of men's relation to each other and to Him. His will is the reuniting of people who have become alienated and enemies to one another. As a result of your experience at home and school and else-where you realize how much estrangement there is among people, and how much reuniting is needed. Such healing and restoration of people to each other calls for a powerful expression of love. But the only vehicle such love has is the attitudes and actions of people who themselves having been accepted are able to give acceptance to others. In this way the understanding, acceptance, and love of God is expressed. Many people do not realize that God appeals to men through men. "We are ambassadors of Christ, God making his appeal through us." If we love God it must mean that we love men. If we love men it must mean we love God. And one most important way we can love God is by loving one another.[1] In these ways we participate in the healing and reuniting work of God.

These thoughts are important in choosing your purposes and work. You might choose a healing profession, such as doctor, nurse, or social worker; or work that arbitrates the relation between men such as management and labor; or personnel work of some kind because of interests in persons. The point is that in such choices you are not only choosing a job but choosing a purpose through which you can participate in a part of the purposes and work of God. The same possibilities exist for all people, whether they are members of the helping professions or not.

A third work of God is the restoration and releasing of the creative powers of men. These powers are released as men work and piece together their knowledge and skill as you would join the pieces of a jig-saw puzzle to make a whole picture. Bill discovered this through his experience as a member of the football team. Astronauts are not able to fly without the strength and skills of all the people that

[1] My own belief is that the only way I can love God that will please Him is by loving my brother who is a child of God; further I know of no way for God to convey His love to me except through the association of men that came into being through Christ who in human form gave all men His love.

contribute to the space enterprise. The realization of your creativity is dependent upon the expression of the creativity of others. The work of education and of government and of scientific and industrial enterprise, in fact, all human activity that brings men together in the accomplishment of all kinds of expression, give individuals opportunity to participate in God's creativity, to receive one's own creative powers, and to make them available to others.

This kind of sense of purpose, with its implicit participation in God's work, is the kind of human activity that will give you power over your negative moods, make their energy and meaning available for constructive purposes, and engender in you the positive moods that can be a part of inspiration and creative effort. In so doing you become a part of something that is immensely bigger than you are in which you find greater room to live and think and plan. Bill, you remember, had an experience of this. "Lately I've begun to think that I can be a part of something tremendous and much bigger than any of us. I want to be a part of it. . . . I want to throw myself into it not caring what happens as long as we play well, and yet wanting to win. . . . But what is winning in this new game that I seem to be joining. Our minister thinks I'm discovering the religious dimension of my life. Maybe . . . I can't follow the church's ideas, but if there's something there I'd like to find it. It's as if some part of me is going to join up with another part of me. I sense an excitement growing within me that makes it impossible to 'play it cool.' I don't want to keep things 'cool.' . . ." Bill is being caught up into something that men call faith, a sense of infinite relationship in which the possibilities of life seem unlimited. Being grasped by this kind of faith makes one seem freer.

But being free means being free to struggle. One of the

struggles is the struggle to find purpose for your life. Your struggles thus have religious meaning. Through them you participate in God's action which he expresses in the world through the decisions and actions of men. Your search for identity and integrity, for instance, is really a religious thing. You are really searching to find the self that you were created to be. Any despair that you feel about yourself can only be understood in relation to your hope of self-realization. Thus your despair about yourself is the negative side of whatever identity and integrity you are achieving. And no one can possibly have a sense of identity and integrity without experiencing despair. Even Jesus Christ, who had a clear sense of who he was, was always being tested by men's denial and persecution of him, which challenged his identity occasionally even, to the point of despair.

Being a child of God means that sometimes you will doubt whether you are one, which means also that you may question whether there is a God in the first place. The more you search for identity and integrity, and the more identity and integrity you achieve, the more sense of struggle you will experience. To whatever degree you have learned to count on yourself, on one another, and on God you have eliminated some moods of self-doubt. Faith helps us to accept self-doubt as being a necessary part of our lives.

Your moods of fear are an expression of your sense of helplessness in the face of some terrifying alternatives. We often get "hung up" on these. I once asked a young person, who was experiencing a real bind between two alternatives, to describe his experience. He drew a picture of a human figure with its arms stretched out, each wrist tied to a post on either side of him. His body made the figure of a cross. It was a picture of helplessness and portrayed the helplessness we all feel when we get strung up between a bind. You experience all kinds of binds. One boy described his as a choice between "a college with no girls and a good education and college where there were girls and fun and only a fair education." Another described his as having to choose between "a girl I am crazy about and my parents, who do not approve of her." The pain of the bind comes when you decide between alternatives. The Cross is a symbol of the suffering, that results when a decision is made that breaks binds. If we can accept our crosses and suffering, we will break out of binds, grow, and conquer. Out of these kinds of experiences you will gather meanings that will help you to understand some of the meanings of the Cross of Christ. Jesus was hung up on the cross because of a bind men were caught in between the alternatives of fear, on the one hand, and love on the other. A part of the message of the Cross is that because Christ allowed himself to be helpless for men's helplessness, he acquired the power to appeal to them through his love, and to lead them in a more courageous and triumphant way of fighting hostile moods and destructive behavior. This faith that calls on potential power even in the midst of seeming defeat and helplessness can free us from the bondage of our depressing moods. We all experience helplessness in the face of problems we cannot solve, and we will always have insoluble problems. The good news is that we need not be destroyed by them.

Again, your resentments and rages, which at times seem so very destructive to you, can be understood to be the negative witnesses to a love that they seem to deny. We can remember that they really are the dark side of love, rather than be a denial of love altogether. In this way moods of resentment and rage will not have such destructive effects. And as we have said earlier, the meaning and energy of these dark moods can be redirected against the real enemies of love.

The wonderful thing about Jesus Christ is that he transformed the destructive forces into constructive ones. This is what "redemption" means, to use a word that you may not like or understand: It means to change what is evil into good. He saw the good and potentially good in everything and everybody and, more, reached out to touch the sick and evil to heal and recreate it. By our trust in him this same power may be ours.

Finally, in the light of this kind of faith, there are answers and helps for the moods that are caused by your sexual preoccupations and erotic crushes. God is not against sex. One young person responded to that statement by asking: "What about sex outside of marriage?" He was thinking of sex as intercourse only. They are not synonymous. Sex is more extensive and fundamental than marital intercourse. There are wide varieties of normal sexual feelings and expressions short of intercourse that are to be expected and accepted. Babies, children, young people, single people all have sex feelings and experiences long before mature sexual expression is possible. To use an analogy, we ride in an automobile long before we are licensed to drive. Likewise, we respond to our sexual feelings for years before we are able to assume the responsibilities of intercourse which are best experienced in marriage. A legitimate part of your experiences as young people are your experiences of attraction to each other, your excitement and passion, your expression of affection which are all necessary, desirable, and important. The only "taboo" is that you do not hold this wonderful gift cheaply and give it away as if it were of no value. The other thing to avoid is the stifling of your love, of your feeling for others, so that it is no longer available to you in either the enterprises of love or of creative work. Your expression of sex must be appropriate to your age and your degree of responsibility. Sexual standards are changing but the fact remains that free sexual expression should not endanger the health and well-being of its participants, or complicate destructively the lives of others, or place babies born of the union in relationships of deprivation. Every privilege requires the exercise of disciplines. When these are observed you may have faith in the wonderfulness and purposefulness of sex. Such an attitude can relieve you of these moods that are often caused by sexual feelings and preoccupations that are often associated with guilt.

It is true, however, that you and your generation will have to work out your own ethical principles for the expression of your passions of soul and body in relation to your purposes, the good of others, and the purposes of God. The old standards by which your parents were raised cannot govern you, but neither are they to be discarded wholesale. They provide you a basis for thinking through your own relation to one another and in the interest of your relationship with God and man.

Conclusion

You will meet God not only in church, but in the daily arena and issues of life, in your successes and failures, in your dealings with men and your struggles with the nature and forces of life. You will meet him, he will speak to you, sometimes in forms that you may not recognize, and you will respond by what you decide, and say, and do. In these meetings you and your moods will be healed and their energies and meanings redirected.